HERE'S TO LIFE

BY

SHARON THOMAS

---

*Welcome to Authentic Greek and Mediterranean
Cuisine featuring the exclusive use of Omega-3
and Omega-9 fatty acids and including
ingredients high in antioxidant value
for optimum health.*

An incredibly nutritious and delicious way to eat.

C.T.S.
ENTERPRISES

I wish to acknowledge "Pier 1 Imports", as many of their fine products were used in the displays of our recipe photographs.

Canadian Cataloguing in Publication Data

Thomas, Sharon,
Here's to Life: traditional Greek and Mediterranean cuisine

Includes index.
ISBN 0-9686634-0-0

1. Cookery, Greek. 2. Cookery, Mediterranean. I. Title.

TX723.5.G8T56 2001   641.59495   C2001-900019-7

Printed and bound by Book Art Inc.,
Scarborough, Ontario, Canada

Book design by Fortunato Design Inc.
Distributed by Hushion House Publishing Inc.
Photography by Stephanie Buchanan

Published by:
C.T.S. Enterprises
P.O. Box 126
Brampton, Ontario
L6V 2K7

TABLE OF CONTENTS

ACKNOWLEDGEMENTS

It is with much gratitude that I acknowledge the following people who were instrumental in the creation of Here's To Life. These are the people without whose valuable help and support, I could not have not done it.

Monica Wright-Roberts, Chairman of the National Breast Cancer Fund, Toronto, Canada, whom I am proud to call my friend, for her support and confidence in me. Monica's tireless efforts have achieved widespread recognition and support for NBCF, which was established to provide direct financial support for breast cancer research and all aspects of the management of the disease, targeting programs across Canada. With sincere thanks.

Andrea R. Martin, Founder and Executive Director, The Breast Cancer Fund, San Francisco, California, for her belief in me, and for her wholehearted support of Here's To Life. Andrea is the founder of The Breast Cancer Fund, an American non-profit organization, created to address the urgent need for a widespread public response to the breast cancer epidemic. With gratitude.

Dr. W. Willett, M.D. Dr.P.H. Professor of Epidemiology and Nutrition and Chair, Department of Nutrition, Harvard School of Public Health, Boston, Massachusetts, for his invaluable research for the good of all women. For his assistance and direction toward the appropriate studies conducted and articles published which were the groundwork for my book. For his numerous accomplishments including his renowned Mediterranean "Diet pyramid" and for all of his efforts and contributions toward finding a cure for breast cancer. I applaud you!

Dr. Dimitrios Trichopoulos, Department of Epidemiology, Harvard School of Public Health, Boston Massachusetts, for his helpful articles on case-controlled studies conducted on the rates of breast cancer and ovarian cancer in Greece and for his extremely informative article on "Traditional Greek Diet and Coronary Heart Disease," as well as numerous other articles which were essential to the research conducted for the nutritional values of the contents of the recipes in Here's To Life. His work has been inspirational!

Susan Haines, RD for her extremely informative and comprehensive introduction to Here's To Life and for her valuable comments on the nutritional value of the traditional Greek and Mediterranean diet and good eating habits in general. My sincere thanks and gratitude for an amazing contribution to my book. It has been a great pleasure to work with Susan!

Stephanie Buchanan, my amazingly talented photographer, for her endless patience and her insistence for detail. Stephanie has the ability to make her camera bring my recipes to life.

Fortunato Aglialoro, for his incredible artistic abilities demonstrated in the design of the cover and the interior of my book.

Esther Penny, Secretary of the National Breast Cancer Fund. Esther's help, knowledge and organizational skills are a constant source of support. Thanks Esther!

Lorraine Crevier, my dear friend and confidant. A breast cancer survivor with more courage and strength than anyone I know. Never too busy with her own life to help. I can always rely on her for valuable opinions, suggestions and genuine concern. Truly a great inspiration. I'm so lucky to know Lorraine.

Last, but not least, my husband, Anthony, and my four children, Joanne, George, Julie and Nadia, for their patience and constructive criticism, but most of all, for their love.

ANDREA R. MARTIN, Founder and Executive Director, *The Breast Cancer Fund* *

What an honor it is to be included in Sharon Thomas' healthy, delicious new cookbook, *Here's To Life*. The recipes in this cookbook endorse what we at *The Breast Cancer Fund* believe to be good for the health of our bodies as well as the planet. This includes eating lower on the food-chain — lots of fruits and vegetables. It also means eating less meat, limiting polyunsaturated fats and increasing your intake of legumes. Based on what we know so far, a diet like the one presented in *Here's To Life* makes sense as part of an overall approach to a healthier lifestyle, and may lower your risk for breast cancer and other illnesses such as heart disease. While shopping for these delicious recipes, also consider buying organic, local produce that is in-season, and most importantly, have fun!

I cannot wait to experiment with these recipes at home and share them with my colleagues, family and friends who care about increasing their well-being while eating well.

MONICA WRIGHT-ROBERTS Chairman, *National Breast Cancer Fund*

As chairman of the *National Breast Cancer Fund*, I'd like to express my hearty support of this cookbook and of its author, Sharon Thomas.

The *National Breast Cancer Fund* is a grassroots organization funding breast cancer initiatives in every province across Canada. We are committed to boosting quality of life for women with breast cancer and for all people! In this way, an approach to healthful eating is an important step.

Sharon has been one of our greatest corporate supporters and we wish her great success with this endeavor. We would also like to thank Sharon and all the readers of this book, as a portion of the proceeds is donated to NBCF, and therefore to making life better for women with breast cancer. For further information, please visit our web site at: www.nbcf.net.

SUSAN HAINES is a Registered Dietician with ten years' experience working in oncology at Princess Margaret Hospital in Toronto, including two years at Princess Margaret Hospital Lodge. Ms. Haines is currently specializing in the areas of breast, lung and esophageal cancers and sits on various hospital committees for the breast site at PMH.

The following pages contain comments, information and professional opinions of Susan Haines, RD. We would like to take this opportunity to sincerely thank Susan Haines, RD for her invaluable addition to *Here's to Life*.

---

* The Breast Cancer Fund is a national advocacy and funding organization based in San Francisco, California that seeks to end the breast cancer epidemic by finding safer, less toxic methods of detection and treatment; uncovering preventable environmental causes of the disease, and ensuring access to the best available medical care and information for everyone. For more information visit www.breastcancerfund.org or call 1-800-487-0492.

INTRODUCTION

It is the author's belief that *Here's To Life* offers everyone the opportunity to become an accomplished Greek and Mediterranean chef with minimal effort. What many perceive as complicated, time-consuming culinary creations will in fact present themselves as easy-to-prepare recipes, not only filled with wonderful, savoury flavors that will delight even the most discriminating pallets, but contain ingredients bursting with nutritional value.

Here's To Life will not only introduce you to traditional Greek and Mediterranean recipes, but will carry these authentic flavors and ingredients forward to a superb array of appetizers and entrees which are certain to please.

Each of the recipes in *Here's To Life* contains the basic ingredients, quantity and combination required to achieve the authentic flavor. No recipe is exact. Everyone's tastes and preferences in foods vary. If one thousand chefs create the same dish, the result will be one thousand delicious variations. No two will be identical. And this is the beauty of cooking. With the exception of the "Breads and Doughs" Section, and of the "Desserts" Section of this book, where exact measurements are essential in order to achieve successful results, personalization of each recipe makes it your very own. Just as the original creators did not own measuring spoons or measuring cups, you too can slightly vary. Sample as you create. If you prefer a specific flavor, add more; if you don't like something, substitute it by using more of another, or just leave it out. The result will be slightly different, but truly your own. The goal is to achieve a flavor which is enjoyable by you and your family and friends. Cooking is not an exact science; it is an artistic expression of one's love of food and of life. In order to be a great chef, one must cook with one's heart. Don't be afraid to experiment – the only ingredient in any successful recipe that can never be omitted is love.

Journey into a new dimension of fabulous foods, or should I say an old dimension? Either way, experience something completely different, with recipes that have been passed down from generation to generation, combining exotic flavors and nutritional value. Let us introduce you to a totally different eating experience that is surprisingly simple to achieve and sure to add spice to your life.

For decades, medical studies have shown that women of the countries of the Mediterranean have had a far lower risk of breast cancer than women of North America. Study after study has shown that women in Mediterranean countries from Spain through Greece come up time and again with low rates of breast cancer. The Greek island of Crete seems to represent the epitome of the healthy Mediterranean diet. No one can know for certain the reasons for these repeated findings. A combination of factors would need to be considered when determining why these women's breast cancer rates are low when compared to the breast cancer rates of North America. A number of factors, such as lifestyle, stress levels, exercise, natural environment, use or non-use of foods treated with insecticides, pesticides and antibiotics, work habits and mental attitude, social interaction, and of course, diet, would all need to be examined.

If one were to consider diet, it would have to be noted that there is an incredible difference between the traditional diet of Greece and the diet of North America. One of the biggest changes in the North American diet during the years that breast cancer risk has risen has been the rise of omega-6 fat consumption. We know these fats by their traditional name "polyunsaturated fats." North Americans have shown the largest increase in consumption of vegetable oils in the world over the past thirty years. Doctors are just beginning to understand the dangers of omega-6 fats. The traditional Greek diet includes the use of omega-3 and omega-9 fatty acids. If these omega-3 and omega-9 fatty acids could be used to specifically replace the use of omega-6 or polyunsaturated fats, possibly overall heath benefits, specifically breast health benefits, could occur.

Omega-6 fats are not part of the traditional Greek diet. These fats are contained in the following: safflower oil, corn oil, soybean oil, peanut oil, cottonseed oil, grapeseed oil, borage oil, primrose oil, sesame oil, foods made with omega-6 fatty acids, such as most commercially bottled mayonnaise and most salad dressings, and of course, margarine. The most prominent foods containing omega-3 fatty acids are fatty, deep cold water fish. Omega-9 fats, best known as "monounsaturated fats," are found in olive oil and canola oil.

The traditional Greek diet is so obviously healthy. It is filled with fresh vegetables, high in fiber and very low in saturated fat. Meat is eaten in relatively small portions. Many of the dishes are not only vegetarian dishes which either feature vegetables or legumes or a combination of both, but are also completely suitable for the vegan diet. The diet contains foods high in antioxidant value such as onions, garlic, eggplant, tomatoes, fresh lemon, paprika, green vegetables, citrus fruit, spinach, cabbage, celery and, of course, olives, olive oil and canola oil. Possibly, adopting a cuisine containing ingredients that have assisted to protect women for generations by deliberately replacing potentially harmful fats, as we know them, with omega-3 fats and omega-9 fats, could be a safe way to approach achieving increased breast health.

DIET AND BREAST CANCER

When Sharon asked me to write some nutrition information on diet and breast cancer and, in particular, the Greek diet in relation to breast cancer, I thought, "What a huge endeavor!" In recent years, this issue has received a lot of attention. New information is coming to light all the time and determining which components of diet are more "breast healthy" is gradually being discovered.

The topic is a large one. Let's use dietary fat as an example. So many questions come to mind. Does too much fat promote breast cancer? If so, how much? Is the type of fat more of an issue? If so, what type? Are both the amount and type of fat important? You can see that there are many aspects to consider. It may seem like we're looking for a needle in a haystack. And it's a big haystack! However, it is worth the effort.

BREAST CANCER RATES AND DIET

A good starting point is to look at the breast cancer rates of people in different regions of the world. In general, breast cancer rates are higher in the developed countries in North America and Europe. The traditional dietary pattern in these regions is one of high fat and low fibre. The developing nations in Africa and Asia have lower breast cancer rates and they traditionally consume diets low in fat and high in fibre.

This trend is not absolute, however; an exception is in the Mediterranean region, including Greece, where the breast cancer rates are low and the dietary fat intake is high (fibre intake is also high).

These observations lead to the investigation of the effects of the different foods. In the nutrition world, we often talk in terms of nutrients or dietary constituents like vitamins and phytochemicals, but people don't eat nutrients. We eat food. And we eat for many reasons: to nourish ourselves, for the enjoyment of eating, and to celebrate special occasions. Therefore, although certain nutrients will be mentioned, I would like our focus to be on food.

Susan Haines, RD

FOODS

Fat

Monounsaturated fat, or omega-9 fatty acid, is found in olive and canola oils, and in avocados. Funnily enough, monounsaturated fat is receiving a lot of attention for what it doesn't do. It seems that it is the most "benign" type of fat, causing no harm. Until recently, Canadians have not included much monounsaturated fat in their diet. In recent years, however, the use of both olive and canola oils has increased.

Saturated fat is mainly found in foods of animal origin, such as meats, poultry, eggs and dairy products. The notable exceptions are the plant sources of saturated fat -coconut and palm oil. In the past, we have typically consumed too much saturated fat, focusing on the higher fat protein foods as the main part of our meals. We also consume too much coconut and palm oil - often without knowing it -in commercially baked goods. With more public awareness of the impact on heart health, the fat content of the Canadian diet has decreased.

Polyunsaturated fat is found in vegetable oils, like corn, sunflower and safflower oils, which provide omega-6 fatty acids to the diet. We typically consume high levels of these oils and cooking oils and in the form of trans-fatty acids. When oils are treated to be solid at room temperature, this process is called hydrogenation. This produces trans-fatty acids, which act like saturated fats. Hydrogenated vegetable oils are commonly used in commercially baked goods, like cookies and crackers. A possible role of these trans-fatty acids in breast cancer development is getting serious attention. It is advisable to reduce the intake of hydrogenated or partially-hydrogenated oils, regardless of which type of oil they are derived from. Ingredient lists on packaged goods will show ingredients in order of highest quantity to lowest. Look for products that do not have a hydrogenated oil in the top three ingredients.

Polyunsaturated fat is also found in flax and fatty fish, such as salmon, which are sources of omega-3 fatty acids. It is thought that a more healthy balance of omega-3 and omega-6 fatty acids is needed. There is now much interest in increasing the amount of omega-3 fatty acids in the diet and decreasing the amount of omega-6 fatty acids as a possible means of reducing breast cancer risk.

A word of caution concerning fat. Lately, there has been an "anti-fat" movement in the public's mind. The public health message to reduce fat intake has been interpreted to mean "cut out all fat." As a result, there has been an explosion of fat-free products on the market, many of which really only provide sugar, refined flour and calories. While the use of these products may indeed reduce fat intake, they do not necessarily improve the quality of the diet. Fat is a necessary ingredient to our diet. We need to ensure, however, that we limit the amount we eat and focus on the better types of fat.

Vegetables

Everything old is new again. Could there be a more familiar expression than "Eat your vegetables!" Now that old expression has some science behind it. In studies on diet and breast cancer risk, a high intake of vegetables has been associated with lower risk. Vegetables provide fibre, vitamins, minerals and phytochemicals. From a "real food" perspective, they provide color and flavor as well. The most nutritious vegetables are the ones that are brightly colored leafy greens like spinach, romaine lettuce and Swiss chard; orange veggies like carrots, sweet potato and squash; red veggies like red pepper, tomatoes and beets.

Fruit

Just like vegetables, although not quite as strong, the evidence is mounting that there is a relationship between high fruit intake and lower breast cancer risk. And, just like veggies, the more colorful, the better; red fruit like grapefruit, strawberries and watermelon; orange fruit like tangerines, mangoes and cantaloupe, purple fruit like grapes and blueberries.

Legumes

To some of us, legumes are quite foreign. To others, they are daily fare. With our multicultural society, there is an opportunity to explore different cuisines. Soy has been studied extensively in relation to reducing breast cancer risk. Soy, which is a legumes, is a major protein source in Asian diets and tofu, a soy product, has found its way onto many Canadian tables. Although the research is inconclusive, other legumes such as lentils, chickpeas, kidney beans, lima beans and fava beans also may prove to be beneficial, possibly due to their high folate content.

Cereals and Whole Grains

For so many reasons, whole grains are superior to refined grains. Examples of whole grain foods are whole wheat bread, brown or wild rice, corn and oatmeal. They supply fibre, B vitamins, and vitamin E. There may be a reduction in breast cancer risk due to these components.

Red Meat

High red meat intake has been cited as a possible risk factor for breast cancer development. This could be due to the large amount of fat that meat can contribute. Or it may be independent of fat content. There are certain cancer-causing compounds, called heterocyclic amines, that are formed when meat is cooked quickly over high heat. Barbecued or grilled meats that are well-done to the point of charring contain higher amounts of these compounds and these cooking methods are very popular in North America.

Fish

Future research will give us more to go on regarding the benefits of fish intake. Right now, there is interest in the omega-3 fatty acids in fish and the possible protective effect against breast cancer development.

Milk and Dairy Products

Well, flip a coin! The research points in both directions, so we really can't come down either way on the effect of milk on breast cancer development. On the negative side, milk can contribute significant amount of fat if whole milk and dairy products are consumed. However, there are lower fat dairy products available, so milk can be included in our diet without adding excessive fat. On the positive side, milk products contain conjugated linoleic acid, yet another food component which is under examination for its possible role in reducing breast cancer risk.

Alcohol

This is an area where the research is quite compelling. Alcohol intake increases breast cancer risk. The higher the intake the greater the cancer risk. This means that two drinks per day increases risk more than one drink per day. There is no evidence that an occasional drink is harmful.

CHARACTERISTICS OF THE TRADITIONAL GREEK DIET

As previously mentioned, one of the lowest breast cancer rates among developed nations is Greece. When looking at the traditional Greek diet, there are eight defining characteristics that may contribute to this phenomenon.

1. *High Monounsaturated to Saturated Fat Ratio.* The major source of fat in the Greek diet is olive oil. This is consumed daily and is used in cooking and as a dressing for salads and vegetables.

2. *High Consumption of Vegetables.* High vegetable intake is a hallmark characteristic of Mediterranean diets. A wide variety of vegetables ensures a broad range of phytochemicals at every meal. Spinach and other leafy greens, tomatoes, sweet bell peppers, cucumbers, carrots, zucchini, eggplant, leeks and okra are just some of the veggies that fill the plate.

3. *Having a piece of fruit is the usual way to end a meal in Greece.* Like vegetables, there are many fruits to choose from. Grapes, strawberries, melons, pears, peaches, oranges, figs, cherries and apricots are samples of the varieties available.

4. *High Consumption of Legumes.* Legumes have been a part of many healthy eating styles and Greek cuisine is no exception. Traditionally, legumes have held a place in most Greek meals as the main course, in soups or as a hot or cold side dish. The commonly eaten legumes in Greece include fava beans, chickpeas, lentils and kidney beans.

5. *High Consumption of Grains.* The Greek diet is characterized by a high consumption of grains. This category includes rice, pasta, whole grain bread and potatoes.

6. *Low Consumption of Meat and Meat Products.* The Greek diet includes all types of meat. However, meat is not consumed every day and when it is, it is often a small com-

ponent of a meal. An example is an entree of red peppers stuffed with beef or lamb or pork and rice. Also, because of proximity to the sea, fish is a significant protein source.

7. *Low Consumption of Milk and Dairy Products.* The main dairy products are feta cheese and yoghurt. Feta is included in many dishes, but relatively small amounts. It is a moderate fat cheese containing 6 grams of fat and 75 calories per ounce. Compare this to the Canadian favorite – cheddar – which contains 9.6 grams of fat and 114 calories per ounce.

8. *Moderate Consumption of Alcohol.* While wine with meals is a defining characteristic of most Mediterranean countries, including Greece, it should be noted that women consume far less alcohol than men, rarely consuming more than a glass per day. This is important in light of the evidence showing increasing breast cancer risk with increasing alcohol consumption.

THE BOTTOM LINE

While the focus of this discussion has been on breast cancer, it is worth noting that the following recommendations are consistent with those for general healthy eating.

• Keep total quantities of fat moderate, 30% or less of total calories.

• Focus on monounsaturates as the main source of fat.

• Use whole grains.

• Increase vegetable intake to three or more servings daily, including leafy greens.

• Increase fruit intake to three or more servings daily.

• Keep meat servings small, about 3 ounces or 90 grams.

• Have some meatless meals where legumes take center stage.

• Include fish in the diet.

• Choose low-fat milk and dairy products.

• Limit alcohol to less than one glass per day.

As I mentioned at the beginning, new information is continually being discovered, and dietary recommendations will evolve with these discoveries. It may be that the answer we're looking for isn't a needle in a haystack after all. Maybe it's the haystack itself. Maybe there is no single dietary component that plays a major causative or preventive role in breast cancer development. Instead, one's diet in total, the day-to-day choices we make, may be the real answer. Variety, balance and moderation. Variety in our fruit, vegetable and whole grain intake, balance in our choice of fats, and moderation in our portion sizes of foods that are high in fat and calories.

Susan Haines, RD

FREQUENTLY USED INGREDIENTS IN GREEK COOKING

FOOD	NUTRIENTS
Feta cheese	• Good source of calcium, necessary for strong bones
Garlic and onion	• Contain allyl sulfides, which are being investigated for possibly reducing the risk for certain cancers and cardiovascular disease
Legumes (peas and beans)	• Good source of folate, a B vitamin • Good source of potassium and phosphorus
Lemon	• Good source of vitamin C, an antioxidant with a role in wound healing • Contains the phytochemical d-limonene, which has anti-cancer properties
Mint and oregano	• Contain flavonoids and other phytochemicals
Olive oil	• Good source of monounsaturated fat • Good source of vitamin E, an antioxidant
Paprika	• Contains carotenoids, which act as antioxidants
Parsley	• Good source of folate • Good source of vitamin A, required for night vision and eye health
Potatoes	• Excellent source of potassium • Good source of vitamin C
Red bell peppers	• High in vitamin C • Contains the carotenoids lutein and zeaxanthin, indicated in reducing the risk of cataracts
Romaine lettuce	• Good source of folate and vitamin A • Contains lutein and zeaxanthin
Spinach	• Good source of folate and vitamin A • Contains lutein and zeaxanthin
Tomato	• Good source of potassium • Good source of vitamin C • Contains the carotenoid lycopene, which is being investigated for possibly reducing risk of certain cancers

Reference Articles

Craig, W.J. Health-promoting properties of common herbs *Am J Clin Nutr* 1999 M(Suppl): 491S-9S

Gandini, S et al. Meta-analysis of studies on breast cancer risk and diet: the role of fruit and vegetable consumption and the intake of associated micronutrients *Euro J Cancer* 2000 36:616-46

James, WPT et al. The mediterrannean diet: protective or simply non-toxic? *Euro J Clin Nutr* 1989 43 (Suppl 2)31-41

Kouris-Blazos, A eta]. Are the advantages of the Mediterranean diet transferable to other populations? A cohort study in Melbourne, *Australia BrJ Nutr* 1999 82:57-61

Levi, F et al. Worldwide patterns of cancer mortality, 1990-1994 *Euro J Cancer Prev* 1999 8:381-400

Potischman, N et al. Intake of food groups and associated micronutrients in relation to risk of early-stage breast cancer *Int J Cancer* 1999 82:3 15-21

Rohan, TE et al. Dietary folate consumption and breast cancer risk *J Natl Cancer Inst* 2000 92(3): 266-9

Ronco, A et al. Vegetables, fruits, and related nutrients and risk of breast cancer: a case-control study in *Uruguay Nutr Cancer* 1999 35(2): 111-9

Trichopoulou, A eta]. The traditional Greek diet *Euro J Clin Nutr* 1993 47 (SuppI I): S76-S78

Trichopoulou, A eta]. Traditional Greek diet and coronary heart disease *J Cardio Risk*, 1994 l(l): 9-15

Trichopoulou, A et al. Diet mid overall survival in elderly people *BMJ* 1995 311:1457-60

Trichopoulou, A et al. Consumption of olive oil and specific food groups in relation to breast cancer risk in Greece *J Natl Cancer Inst* 1995 87(2):110-6

Zhang, S et al. Dietary carotenoids and vitamins A. C, and E and risk of breast cancer *J Natl Cancer Inst* 1999 91(6): 547-56

Zheng, W et al. Well-done meat intake and the risk of breast cancer *J Natl Cancer Inst* 1998 90(22): 1224-9

Reference Books

A Perfect 10. Phytonutrients against Cancer. by L. Pawlak. 1998 Biomed General Corp

Food, Nutrition and the Prevention of Cancer: a global perspective. World Cancer Research Fund and American Institute for Cancer Research 1997

Never Underestimate The Power of A Lemon

Perhaps what makes the flavors of Greek foods so unique and different from any others, is the repeated use of fresh lemon. Almost every dish is commonly accompanied by a wedge of lemon or two or three. It is traditional to squeeze lemon on just about everything they eat. It would not be uncommon to squeeze fresh lemon over rice dishes, potatoes, fish, Iamb, chicken, pork and even dishes which already contain lemon such as salads, legumes and vegetable spreads. In restaurants, savory dishes are always served with fresh lemon and in Greek homes, lemon is a staple.

Nutritional value is no doubt added to the daily Greek diet through the repeated use of fresh lemon juice. We know that lemons add zesty flavor to our North American drinks, but if one were to acquire a taste for fresh lemon as a condiment, imagine the health benefits. Lemons are high in antioxidant value. Look what we would be adding to our daily diets with just a little squeeze.

HERE'S TO LIFE

Appetizers

SPINACH AND CHEESE DIP WITH FRESH DILL AND OLIVE OIL

1	package fresh spinach, washed and chopped	
1/2 cup	very finely chopped shallots or green onions	125 mL
1 cup	ricotta cheese	250 mL
1 cup	crumbled feta cheese	250 mL
1/4 cup	fresh finely chopped dill weed	62.5 mL (approximately)
1/2 tsp	fresh ground black pepper	2.46 mL
2 tbsp	extra virgin olive oil	29.58 mL
	whole wheat pita bread	

METHOD:

1. Wash and chop fresh spinach. Steam until soft. Drain and cool. Squeeze out all excess water from spinach.

2. Place spinach in a large bowl and add chopped shallots, ricotta and feta cheeses. Add fresh ground pepper and chopped dill weed. Blend all ingredients.

3. Place in a serving dish and garnish with olive oil.

4. Surround spinach and cheese dip with toasted whole wheat pita wedges.

EXOTIC CAVIAR DIP

1 jar	tarama (purchased at any Greek grocery specialty store) (also known as caviar)	
10	slices white sliced bread (crusts removed)	
1/4 cup	cold very soft mashed white potatoes (no milk or butter added)	62.5 mL
	juice from 2 fresh lemons, to taste (not bottled)	
2 tbs.	finely grated white onion	29.58 mL
1/2 cup	canola oil or light olive oil	125 mL
	fresh dill weed for garnish	

METHOD:

1. Place tarama (caviar) in a strainer and rinse with cold water to remove excess salt. Drain completely

2. Place tarama in a mixing bowl and beat with electric beater at high speed. Add oil very gradually. Add grated onion. Continue beating. Add bread, one slice at a time. Add mashed potatoes gradually. Add fresh lemon juice and continue beating until consistency is light and fluffy. Finished dip will have consistency of mayonnaise. If mixture appears too dry, add cold water a few drops at a time.

3. Place dip in a serving bowl and garnish with chopped fresh dill weed. Sprinkle with extra fresh lemon juice if desired. Dip should have a distinct lemony taste. Surround with toasted pita bread wedges or thinly sliced crusty Greek bread.

SPICY PORK AND LEEK COCKTAIL MEATBALLS

3 lb	lean ground pork	1 kg
3	stalks fresh leeks (white part of leeks only) chopped very finely	
2 tsp	fresh ground black pepper	10 mL
2 tsp	Hungarian paprika	10 mL
2 tsp	oregano flakes	10 mL
2 tsp	crushed chili pepper flakes and seeds (hot)	10 mL
2 tsp	salt (optional)	10 mL
2 tbsp	butter	29.58 mL
	olive oil	

METHOD:

1. In a non-stick skillet containing melted butter, sauté finely chopped leeks for approximately 5 minutes, until leeks are tender and beginning to turn brown on the edges. Add paprika, black pepper, oregano flakes and salt. Add crushed chili pepper flakes.

2. In a large bowl, place lean pork. Add sautéed leeks and spices. Mix all ingredients together well. Shape small meatballs in your hand about the size of a walnut. Sauté over medium heat in a non-stick pan lightly brushed with olive oil until meatballs are golden brown and juices run clear.

3. Place on a platter with cocktail toothpicks. Great with hummus dip or on their own. They're spicy!

Ground Lamb Cocktail Meatballs with Cracked Wheat and Toasted Pine Nuts

2 lb	fresh ground local lamb (lean)	1 kg
1 cup	very finely chopped white onion	250 mL
1/4 cup	softened fine cracked wheat (bulgur)	62.5 mL
3 tsp	ground allspice	15 mL
2 tsp	ground cinnamon powder	10 mL
2 tsp	fresh ground black pepper	10 mL
1/4 cup	chopped toasted pine nuts (pan toasted in 2 tbsp or 29.58 mL butter)	62.5 mL
	olive oil	

Method:

1. Place 1/4 cup or 62.5 mL fine cracked wheat (bulgur) in a bowl and add warm water. Rinse and replace water. Be sure the water covers the grain. Allow to stand at room temperature for about a 1/2 hour or until cracked wheat is completely soft and fluffy. Should not be crunchy. If crunchy, allow to stand until softened.

2. In a large bowl, combine ground lamb, chopped onion and spices. Add toasted pine nuts and the butter they were toasted in. Completely squeeze out the softened cracked wheat by hand and add to mixture. Combine all ingredients and form small meatballs the size of walnuts. Brown in olive oil in a non-stick pan until golden brown and juices run clear.

3. Serve on a platter with cocktail toothpicks. Great with tzatziki dip or on their own.

GOAT CHEESE, BLACK OLIVE AND FRESH ROSEMARY FOCACCIA BREAD

Basic pita dough recipe for focaccia

3 cloves	fresh crushed garlic	
1/4 cup	fresh rosemary leaves, stems removed	60 mL
3/4 cup	calamata olives, remove pits and cut in half	180 mL
1 cup	goat cheese (feta cheese may be substituted)	250 mL
1/3 cup	extra virgin olive oil	80 mL
1/2 tsp	salt	3 mL

PITA DOUGH RECIPE
METHOD:

1. Prepare pita (focaccia) dough recipe (see Breads and Dough section). Press out by hand onto a 16-inch (45 cm) round pizza pan, or equivalent.

2. Finely chop fresh rosemary leaves and combine with fresh crushed garlic, olive oil and salt. Brush the top of the focaccia dough, evenly with all of the mixture.

3. Distribute the olives, evenly over the surface of the focaccia. Crumble the cheese evenly.

4. Allow to proof in the pan for 20 minutes before baking. Bake at 350° F or 175° C for about 20 minutes or until the bottom of the crust and the top is beginning to turn a golden brown color. Remove from the oven and allow to stand for about ten minutes before slicing.

5. When served on its own with your choice of salad, this focaccia bread makes a great meal. It may also be cut into bit-size pieces and served as appetizers.

TRADITIONAL GREEK MEATBALLS
(COCKTAIL SIZE)

2 lb	extra lean ground lamb or beef	1 kg
4 slices	white bread, soaked in cold water and squeezed dry	
2 tsp	fresh ground black pepper	10 mL
1 1/2 tsp	salt (optional)	7 mL
1 clove	fresh garlic, crushed	
3/4 cup	finely chopped white onion	185 mL
2	whole eggs	
1/2 cup	finely chopped fresh mint leaves	125 mL
1 cup	white or whole wheat flour	250 mL
4 tbsp	olive oil (for frying)	60 mL

METHOD:

1. In a large bowl, combine all ingredients, except flour and olive oil.

2. Blend together first with a wooden spoon and then by hand until mixture is completely combined. Take a small amount of mixture in the palm of your hand, about the size of a walnut and roll to make a meatball shape. Dredge the meatball on all sides in flour and sauté in a non-stick pan brushed with olive oil. Sauté for about 15 minutes, turning regularly to ensure even browning over moderate heat. Meatballs are done when golden brown and juices run clear.

3. Serve on cocktail toothpicks. Delicious with tzatziki, eggplant, egg and lemon dip, or great on their own.

TRADITIONAL EGG AND LEMON SAUCE (DIP)

3	egg yolks	
1/4 cup	fresh squeezed lemon juice	60 mL
1/4 cup	water	60 mL
1 tbsp	cornstarch	15 mL
1/4 cup	heavy cream (optional)	125 mL
1 cup	chicken or vegetable stock	250 mL
1/4 tsp	salt(optional)	1 mL
	dash of nutmeg (optional)	

METHOD:

1. Beat egg yolks and lemon juice using a wire whisk until light and fluffy.

2. In a separate bowl, blend cool water with cornstarch to make a smooth paste and pour into egg yolk and lemon mixture. Blend thoroughly using the whisk.

3. Transfer mixture to the top of a double boiler and whisk rapidly and constantl over medium heat. Gradually add the stock, always continuing to whisk until the mixture thickens and reaches a creamy smooth consistency. Ensure that mixture is not heated too rapidly and do not allow it to boil, This slow cooking process, together with the rapid whisking motion, prevents the egg yolk from cooking. Slowly add the cream and incorporate it into the sauce until blended. Add salt and nutmeg. Remove from heat.

4. This is a traditional Greek sauce which is commonly used with a variety of dishes. Often, it is served with Greek meatballs and grapevine leaves stuffed with rice. Where stock is required, chicken or vegetable stock may be used.

5. When serving cocktail size meatballs, stuffed grapevine leaves or roasted Greek potatoes as appetizers, egg and lemon sauce may be served as an accompaniment or dip.

Tzatziki Dip

2 cups	plain, unflavored yoghurt	500 mL
1 cup	regular or low fat sour cream	150 mL
1	freshcucumber or $^1/_2$ English cucumber	
2	cloves fresh garlic, crushed	
2 tbsp	olive oil	30 mL
$^1/_2$ tsp	salt (optional)	2.5 mL
1 tbsp	fresh dill weed, finely chopped	15 mL

Method:

1. In a large bowl, combine yoghurt, sour cream, crushed garlic olive oil and salt.

2. Partially peel (creating a striped effect) and finely chop cucumber and add to yoghurt and sour cream mixture. Combine thoroughly.

3. Spoon into a serving dish and garnish with chopped fresh dill weed.

4. May be served with toasted or plain pita bread wedges or used as a dip for fresh vegetables or souvlaki.

HUMMUS DIP

3 cups	cooked chick-peas	750 mL
3 tbsp	sesame seed purée (tahini) (available at Greek and Middle Eastern Grocery Stores)	
4	cloves crushed fresh garlic	
$^1/_5$ cup	fresh squeezed lemon juice (not bottled)	50 mL
1 tsp	salt (optional)	5 mL
2 tbsp	olive oil	30 mL
$^1/_4$ tsp	Hungarian paprika or cayenne powder	1.25 mL
1 tsp	fresh chopped parsley leaves	5 mL

METHOD:

1. Place cooked chick-peas in a food processor. Reserve the water they were cooked in and about six whole chick-peas for decoration. Chick peas should be warm— not cold—when making this dish.

2. Add fresh lemon juice, crushed garlic, salt (optional) and half of the olive oil. Purée on high speed for about 3 minutes until mixture becomes smooth and creamy. Add tahini and continue to blend for an additional 3 minutes. Mixture should have a very smooth and creamy texture and should have a slightly runny or pourable consistency. If mixture is too dry, add reserved liquid very gradually in small amounts until required consistency is achieved. Mixture will thicken as it cools.

3. Taste hummus and add more lemon to taste. This dish should have a distinct lemony taste.

4. Pour into a flat decorative dish and create a swirling design with the back of a large spoon, making smooth crevasses. Place the six whole chick-peas in the center and drizzle with remaining olive oil. To garnish, you may sprinkle with paprika, cayenne pepper and/or a small amount of fresh chopped parsley.

5. Delicious when served with plain or toasted pita bread wedges or as a dip for an array of fresh crunchy bite-size vegetables, e.g. carrots, radishes, broccoli, cauliflower, green, red and yellow peppers, unpeeled zucchini strips and whole mushrooms.

Simple Two Bean Dip

1 cup	cooked white navy beans	250 mL
1 cup	cooked red kidney beans	250 mL
	(all white beans may be used)	
2	cloves fresh, crushed garlic	
$^1/_2$ cup	finely chopped green onions	125 mL
$^1/_4$ cup	finely chopped fresh parsley	60 mL
2 tbsp	extra virgin olive oil	30 mL
1 tbsp	fresh lemon juice (not bottled)	15 mL

Method:

1. In a food processor, place cooked kidney beans and crushed garlic. Garlic should be crushed before adding to beans. Add half of the olive oil and all of the lemon juice. Add chopped green onions and blend.

2. Remove from the food processor and place in a dip bowl. Sprinkle with remaining olive oil and chopped parsley.

3. Serve with pita bread, fresh vegetables, crusty bread rounds, or use as a dip for mini souvlakis.

ROASTED RED PEPPERS AND TOMATOES CANAPÉS WITH CRUMBLED FETA CHEESE

1 cup	roasted sweet red bell peppers, chopped	250 mL
1 cup	ripe red tomatoes, chopped	250 mL
2 tbsp	finely chopped fresh mint	30 mL
2	large cloves of crushed garlic	
2 tbsp	extra virgin olive oil	
1 tsp	fresh squeezed lemon juice (not bottled)	5 mL
1/2 cup	feta cheese, finely crumbled	125 mL
	toasted Greek or Italian bread cut into small pieces.	

METHOD:

1. Place red peppers on a non-stick baking sheet and place under the broiler for about 45 minutes, turning often. Exterior layer of skin will become blackened and dry. Ensure that the oven temperature is not too hot as the peppers will disintegrate rather than roast if temperature is too high.

2. Remove from oven and cool. Peel outer charred skin off; if peppers are cool, the skin will come off easily. If you wish, you may place hot peppers in a plastic bag which helps to separate the blackened skin.

3. Chop peeled, cooled peppers finely and add chopped tomatoes. Add crushed garlic, chopped mint, olive oil and lemon juice. Combine all ingredients, cover tightly and place in the refrigerator until ready to serve. When ready to serve, remove from refrigerator and mix again.

4. Spoon onto toasted bread pieces and garnish with crumbled feta cheese. Arrange on a decorative platter and serve immediately.

Note: Hot banana peppers may be substituted for sweet red bell peppers or they may be combined. If using hot banana peppers, end result will be a hot and spicy flavor.

Sautéed Chicken Liver and Bacon Paté with Caramelized Onions

1 1/2 lb	fresh chicken livers	675 grams
1/2 lb	bacon, well done, fat drained	225 grams
1 cup	white onion, cut in slivers	250 mL
1 1/2 tsp	fresh ground black pepper	7.5 mL
3 tbsp	canola oil	45 mL
1/4 cup	fresh chopped parsley	60 mL

Method:

1. Place chicken livers in water and bring to a boil. Simmer over moderate heat for about a 1/2 hour or until cooked and tender.

2. Cut bacon into small pieces and sauté in a non-stick pan until slightly crisp. Drain on paper towel to remove all excess fat.

3. Brown onions in a non-stick pan in half of the canola oil until they become soft and begin to turn golden brown on the edges. Do not overcook.

4. In a food processor, combine cooked chicken livers, bacon and onions. Add the remainder of the canola oil. Blend for 3 to 5 minutes or until mixture becomes smooth and creamy and spreadable.

5. Place paté in a decorative serving bowl and garnish with chopped fresh parsley and surround with toasted pita bread wedges.

Note: The bacon may be omitted from this recipe if desired.

TANGY ROASTED EGGPLANT DIP WITH FRESH CRUSHED WALNUTS

1	large eggplant or 2 small eggplants	
4 tbsp	sesame seed puree (tahini)	60 mL
1 tsp	salt (optional)	5 mL
1/4 cup	fresh squeezed lemon juice (not bottled)	60 mL
4	cloves crushed garlic (less garlic may be used)	
1/4 cup	finely chopped fresh shelled walnuts (not packaged)	60 mL
2 tbsp	extra virgin olive oil	30 mL
1/2 cup	fresh chopped parsley	125 mL

METHOD:

1. Wash eggplant(s) and pierce with a knife in two or three locations. This is done so that the eggplant will not explode during the cooking process.

2. Wrap eggplant(s) tightly in aluminum foil. The foil keeps the juices in and promotes faster cooking. Bake at 450° F or 225° C for about 45 minutes until eggplant is completely soft and limp. Remove from oven, unwrap and cool.

3. Slit the eggplant with a sharp knife and remove the pulp from one half. Discard the skin from half of the eggplant and use the other half. Place the pulp from the eggplant and half of the skin in a food processor. Add the tahini, crushed garlic and lemon juice. Blend for about 3 minutes until smooth and creamy. Add half of the oil and the chopped parsley. Blend for another half a minute.

4. Spoon creamy eggplant dip onto a decorative dish and sprinkle with remaining olive oil. Garnish with finely chopped walnuts.

5. Serve as a dip with toasted pita bread wedges or with fresh vegetables.

EGGPLANT, SWEET ROASTED RED PEPPER AND TOMATO FOCACCIA CANAPÉS

1	small eggplant, cut into 1/4 inch slices (unpeeled)	
1	large sweet red bell pepper, roasted and cut into thin strips	
1/2 cup	pitted, calamata olives, cut in half (not canned)	125 mL
2 cups	finely chopped fresh ripe tomatoes	500 mL
3 tbsp	extra virgin olive oil	45 mL
2	cloves crushed garlic	
1 tsp	salt (optional)	5 mL
1/3 cup	fresh, finely chopped oregano	80 mL
2 cups	crumbled feta cheese	500 mL

PITA DOUGH RECIPE
METHOD:

1. Prepare pita (focaccia) dough recipe (see Breads and Dough section). Press out by hand onto a 16-inch or 18-inch (50 or 45 cm) round pizza pan.

2. Combine olive oil and crushed garlic and brush this mixture over the top of the dough.

3. Wash and thinly slice eggplant (unpeeled) and brown in a non-stick pan until golden brown on both sides. Remove from heat and cool. Roast peppers and slice into thin strips.

4. Arrange toppings evenly over dough, starting with chopped tomatoes. Tomatoes may be thinly sliced instead of chopped, if preferred. Top with crumbled feta cheese and sprinkle with fresh chopped oregano. Allow to proof in pan for about 20 minutes befpre baking. Bake at 350° F or 175° C for about 20 minutes or until crust is golden brown on the bottom and at the edges. Do not overcook. Remove from oven and cool slightly.

5. Cut into bite-size pieces and arrange on a platter. Serve immediately.

SUCCULENT STUFFED SIRLOIN AND CRACKED WHEAT KEBABS

2 1/4 lb	lean ground top sirloin or (eye of the round) beef (best results come from fine grinding meat, yourself)	1 kg
1 cup	raw cracked wheat	250 mL
3/4 cup	white onion, puréed in food processor	185 mL
1/2 tsp	salt (optional)	2.5 mL
1 tsp	fresh ground black pepper	5 mL
2 tsp	fresh ground allspice powder	10 mL
1 tsp	fresh ground cinnamon powder	5 mL
1	clove fresh crushed garlic	
1 cup	white or whole wheat flour	250 mL

Filling

1/2 lb	lean, coarsely ground top sirloin or (eye of the round)	225 grams
1/2 cup	finely chopped white onion	125 mL
1/4 cup	chopped, toasted pine nuts (pan toasted in 1 tbsp or 15 mL butter) Sunflower seeds may be substituted.	65 mL
1 tsp	salt (optional)	5mL
1 tsp	fresh ground black pepper	5 mL
2 tsp	fresh ground allspice powder	10 mL
2 tsp	fresh ground cinnamon powder	10 mL
2 tbsp	olive oil	30 mL

METHOD:

1. Place cracked wheat in a bowl and add about 3 cups of warm water. Mix water and cracked wheat by hand. Water will become cloudy. Discard cloudy water and add 4 cups of fresh warm water. Be sure all impurities are removed from cracked wheat and discard second water. When cracked wheat is clean, add 3 cups of warm water and allow to stand for about a 1/2 hour or until cracked wheat is very soft and fluffy.

2. To use softened cracked wheat, it must be removed from water by hand and thoroughly squeezed dry before adding to any recipe.

3. Combine all ingredients of the filling in a non-stick pan and sauté over high heat until meat is browned and onions begin to caramelize. Mixture should be completely cooked. Remove from heat and cool.

4. Place 2 1/4 lb or 1 kg of finely ground meat into a large bowl. Add all of the thoroughly squeezed dry softened cracked wheat. Add puréed onion, crushed garlic and spices. Mix thoroughly by hand. The mixture should be sticky but not dry. You should be able to shape mixture easily without it breaking apart. If too dry, add a few drops of cold water until required consistency is reached. Take enough of the meat mixture in your hand to make a ball the size of a lime.

5. Flatten the mixture in the palm of one hand, using the other hand to form a small circular shape, making sure to keep an approximately thickness of about 1/4 inch or just about 1/2 cm. Spoon a heaping teaspoon of the filling into the center of the circle, keeping it in the palm of your hand.

6. Carefully bring the edges of the circle together and close, forming a slightly oval shape. Continue to shape the kebab until the exterior is sealed and smooth. Wet hands with a few drops of cold water to assist in the shaping process and to avoid sticking problems. Kebab must be sealed properly or filling will fall out during cooking process.

7. This method is not difficult, once you get the hang of it. Continue this process until all of the meat and cracked wheat mixture and filling are used

8. Lightly dredge each individual kebab in flour before browning. This helps to keep them sealed and promotes even browning. Sauté kebabs in a non-stick pan, over medium heat, turning regularly, using canola oil for frying. Use tongs to turn kebabs. Cooking time should be approximately 10 minutes or until golden brown.

9. Remove from pan and place on paper towels to remove excess fat. Serve hot or cold. Served on a decorative platter with a hummus dip, they are amazing as a canapé or as part of a meal. Take your bows!

The lean beef in this recipe, both in the outer layer and the filling, may be substituted by lean (local) lamb.

CRUNCHY BITE-SIZE ROASTED GREEK POTATOES

12	large, white potatoes	
4 tbsp	olive oil	60 mL
1 tsp	salt (optional)	5 mL
2 tbsp	dry oregano flakes	30 mL
1 tbsp	Hungarian paprika powder	15 mL
1 tbsp	garlic powder (not garlic salt)	15 mL
1 tsp	fresh crushed black pepper	15 mL
2 tbsp	fresh lemon juice (not bottled)	30 mL

METHOD:

1. Peel and wash potatoes. Ensure that all potatoes are approximately the same size. Cut large potatoes in half and sculpt and round the edges in order to achieve a common shape and size. Prepare about 24 small potatoes, each about the size of a lime.

2. In a large bowl, combine olive oil, salt (optional), oregano flakes, paprika, crushed garlic, black pepper and fresh lemon juice. Add washed and drained potatoes and mix by hand until potatoes are completely and evenly coated.

3. Arrange coated potatoes in a greased shallow casserole dish (not on a cookie sheet). A non-stick casserole dish works well. Place under broiler in a hot oven. Broil until tops become a deep golden brown color. Shut off broiler and bake at about 350° F or 175° C for about 20 minutes or until crispy on the outside and soft on the inside. Potatoes may be turned occasionally, using tongs, if desired, to achieve even browning.

4. Arrange cooked potatoes on a platter. Additional fresh lemon juice may be squeezed over the dish if desired. A delicious accompaniment to any meal and great as an appetizer.

ABOUT PHYLLO DOUGH

Phyllo dough comes frozen at most grocery stores. It is also readily available at all Greek and Mediterranean specialty stores. It is packaged in a long tube-like box and vacuum-packed in plastic to ensure freshness. Phyllo dough must be kept soft at all times during the preparation process. If the dough hardens, it becomes brittle and breaks and is impossible to use.

When choosing phyllo dough, one must experiment with several different brand names. Some are better than others. Some just do not work well. There are a few qualities the phyllo must possess in order to be classified as a "good" dough to use and one which will ensure optimum results for all recipes containing phyllo dough. The phyllo should not be clear or transparent. It should have a dull, dusty white color and should appear non-transparent. The dough should rise during the baking process. It should puff up and expand when exposed to oven heat. If it simply dries out and cracks during the baking process, it is not the correct dough to choose. It should begin to turn a light golden color as it rises, almost immediately after being placed in a hot oven. If this does not take place, try another brand. When you find the phyllo that delivers the best results you will find all of your phyllo recipes will not only be more successful in their baking behaviors, but your recipe will achieve the desired flavor. The phyllo makes the difference.

Phyllo dough can be shaped in many different ways. It can be shaped into triangles, tubes or strudel, diamond-cut shapes or it may be used as a bottom and top crust to form a pie effect. No matter which way phyllo is shaped, it is exceptionally attractive as well as offering uniqueness and elegance in presentation with any of the chosen stuffings.

Stuffed phyllo may be served as an appetizer in bite-size pieces, either hot or cold. It may be prepared in advance and either frozen or refrigerated and heated just before serving. If served as a main course, stuffed phyllo is traditionally accompanied by plain unflavored yoghurt or tzatziki.

When reheating after pastry has cooled or has been in the refrigerator, place individual pieces on a non-stick cookie sheet. Do not overlap. Bake in a moderate oven for 5 - 7 minutes checking regularly to ensure they do not burn. They will become light and flaky when reheated. If frozen phyllo is being reheated, allow for thawing before reheating. Serve hot or cold on a decorative platter as a delicious and unique appetizer. If serving as a main dish, again hot or cold, don't forget the yoghurt or tzatziki. Yummy!

DELECTABLE STUFFED PHYLLO PASTRY

Phyllo pastry is stuffed with a variety of traditional fillings. The method of preparation is always the same; only the fillings change. However, each different filling seems to create a uniquely individual dish and taste experience. I will begin by giving the ingredients to create the traditional varieties of fillings used in Greece for stuffed phyllo pastry. Don't be afraid to create your own filling ideas.

Feta Stuffed Phyllo

1 ¹/2 lb	feta cheese, coarsely crumbled	675 grams
¹/2 lb.	ricotta cheese	225 grams
1 tsp	salt (optional)	5 mL
2	large eggs, slightly beaten	

Method:

Combine cheeses, salt (optional) and eggs in a bowl. Blend well.

Spinach and Feta Stuffed Phyllo

1 lb	feta cheese,coarsely crumbled	450 grams
1 lb	ricotta cheese	450 grams
2 cups	cooked, drained and squeezed dry fresh spinach	500 mL
2	eggs, slightly beaten	
¹/4 cup	finely chopped fresh dill weed	60 mL

Method:

Combine cheeses, drained spinach, eggs and chopped dill in a bowl. Blend well.

GROUND SIRLOIN AND WHITE ONION STUFFED PHYLLO

1 ¹/₂ lb	top sirloin of beef (medium ground)	675 grams
1 cup	finely chopped white onion	250 mL
¹/₄ cup	finely chopped sweet green bell pepper	60 mL
¹/₄ cup	finely chopped sweet red bell pepper	60 mL
¹/₄ cup	toasted pine nuts (optional)	60 mL
1 ¹/₄ cup	chopped stewed tomatoes	300 mL
2	cloves crushed garlic	
¹/₂ tsp	salt (optional)	3 mL
1 tsp	fresh ground black pepper	5 mL
2 tbsp	extra virgin olive oil	30 mL

METHOD:

1. Brown ground meat in olive oil. Add chopped onion, peppers and toasted pine nuts. (Pine nuts may be pan toasted in 1 tbsp or 15 mL butter). Add crushed garlic. Cook until juices of meat run clear and onions are transparent.

2. Add spices and chopped tomatoes. Blend and simmer over medium heat for about 5 minutes, stirring occasionally. Remove from heat and set aside to cool.

Leek and Feta Stuffed Phyllo

2 cups	finely chopped fresh leeks (use white part only)	500 mL
1 lb	feta cheese, crumbled	450 grams
1 lb	ricotta cheese	450 grams
2	eggs, slightly beaten	
1 tsp	salt (optional)	5 mL
2 tbsp	extra virgin olive oil	30 mL

Method:

1. Thoroughly wash and chop leeks (be sure to remove all sand). Sauté leeks in a skillet containing olive oil until they begin to turn golden brown around the edges. Remove from heat and cool to room temperature.

2. In a large bowl, combine sautéed leeks, feta cheese, ricotta cheese, eggs and salt (optional). Refrigerate until ready to use in phyllo pastry.

Squash Stuffed Phyllo

3 cups	cooked, drained and mashed butternut squash or sweet potatoes	750 mL
3	eggs, slightly beaten	
3 tbsp	melted butter	45 mL
1 tsp	white granulated sugar (if using sweet potatoes, sugar is optional)	5 mL

Method:

In a large bowl, combine cooked, mashed squash with eggs, melted butter and sugar. Mixture should have the consistency of mashed potatoes.

PORK TENDERLOIN STUFFED PHYLLO

3/4 lb	lean ground pork	350 grams
3/4 lb	lean pork tenderloin, chopped finely,	350 grams
	(this adds texture to the filling)	
2 tbsp	olive oil or butter	30 mL
2 tbsp	Hungarian paprika	30 mL
3/4 cup	finely chopped sweet red bell pepper	180 mL
1/2 tsp	fresh ground black pepper	2.5 mL
1/2 cup	finely chopped white onion	125 mL
1 tsp	salt (optional)	5 mL
1	egg, slightly beaten	

METHOD:

1. Cut tenderloin into very small pieces; a food processor may be used for this. Place chopped tenderloin and lean ground pork together in a large skillet and brown in butter or olive oil. Cook until meat is tender and juices run clear.

2. Add paprika, black pepper, chopped onions and peppers. Add salt (optional). Blend thoroughly. Remove from heat and cool. Keep refrigerated until ready to use and just before stuffing phyllo, add beaten egg to meat mixture and blend well. The egg will act as a binder during baking.

METHOD FOR STUFFED PHYLLO TUBES TO STRUDEL STYLE

1. Phyllo should be at room temperature when being stuffed in order to allow maximum manipulation of the pastry for all shapes. Phyllo waiting to be used should be kept covered with plastic at all times to ensure softness. If phyllo dries out it will break and is not usable.

2. Use two phyllo sheets at a time for tube method. Brush the entire surface of the phyllo sheets with melted butter.

3. Place about 6 tbsp of filling primarily along the bottom end of the sheets.

4. Roll the pastry in a jelly-roll fashion from bottom to top to form a tube or strudel shape. Carefully lift the stuffed tube and place on a buttered baking dish. Do not use a cookie sheet. Repeat this procedure until all the phyllo dough and all the filling has been used. Place the tubes side by side in the pan, just barely touching each other. Do not crowd or overfill the pan. If necessary, use a second pan. Allow space for tubes to rise during the baking process.

5. Generously brush the tops of the tubes with melted butter. Cover with a clean cloth and allow to stand at room temperature for about 20 minutes before baking. Bake in a 350 degree F or 175 degree C oven for approximately 30 to 45 minutes or until phyllo turns golden brown. Check occasionally to avoid overcooking but do not open the oven for the first 20 minutes.

6. Remove from oven and cover with a clean towel during the cooling process. This ensures that the phyllo remains flaky but does not dry out and become brittle. When cool, the tubes may be cut diagonally to create diamond shapes. If being used for canapés, cut in smaller pieces. If being served as a main dish, the pieces may be larger.

HOMEMADE SAVORY CHEDDAR, EGG AND ONION PITAS

1	portion basic pita dough recipe	
3 cups	coarsely shredded unprocessed cheddar cheese (mild, medium or old may be used)	750 mL
2 tbsp	finely grated white onion	30 mL
3	large eggs, well beaten	
	salt and pepper to taste	
2 tbsp	extra virgin olive oil	30 mL

METHOD:

1. Combine shredded cheese and eggs in a large bowl. Add grated onion and salt and pepper to taste. Combine all ingredients.

2. Divide prepared pita dough into equal portions each the size of a large lemon. Roll out on a well-floured board with a rolling pin in circles of about 5 - 6 in. or 12 - 15 cm. in diameter. Brush surface with olive oil. Place about 2 tbsp or 30 mL of cheese and onion mixture on each circle and spread evenly almost to the edges. More mixture may be used if desired.

3. Bake in a lightly greased baking pan, such as a pizza pan, for about 10 - 15 minutes at approximately 350° F or 175° C until golden brown on the bottom and around the edges. Do not over bake.

4. Remove from oven and serve hot or cold. Great as an accompaniment to any meal or as a main dish with your choice of salad. These pitas may also be made smaller and served as delicious canapés.

Mini Sweet Red Bell Pepper and Feta Triangles

2 cups	sweet red bell pepper, finely chopped	500 mL
1 lb	feta cheese, crumbled	450 grams
1/2 cup	finely chopped parsley	125 mL
2	eggs, slightly beaten	
2 tbsp	extra virgin olive oil	30 mL
1/2 tsp	salt (optional)	3 mL
1	package commercial phyllo dough	
1/4 cup	melted butter for brushing	60 mL

Method:

1. Sauté peppers in olive oil over medium heat for approximately two minutes or until they just begin to soften. Do not brown. Remove from heat and cool to room temperature.

2. Combine sautéed peppers, feta cheese, chopped parsley and eggs in a bowl. Add salt (optional).

3. Prepare phyllo dough for triangles (as per recipe on page 30). Cut strips in two-inch widths. Brush the surface of each strip with melted butter.

4. Allow 1 tsp or 5 mL of filling per triangle. Fold each phyllo strip to form a triangle shape. Continue this procedure until all of the phyllo and all of the filling is used. Place triangles on a lightly buttered baking dish and brush the tops, evenly with melted butter. Bake at 350° F or 175° C for approximately 15 minutes or until golden brown and puffy.

5. Remove from heat and serve on a decorative platter as delicious canapés. This recipe may also be made using the tube or strudel shape phyllo dough method.

SPICY MINI COCKTAIL KEBABS (SOUVLAKI)

2 lb	chicken breast or lean pork (cut into $1/2$ inch or $1 \ 1/2$ cm. cubes)	2 kg
$1/4$ cup	olive oil	60 mL
4 tsp	dry oregano flakes	20 mL
1 tsp	dry mint	5 mL
1 tsp	salt (optional)	5 mL
2 tsp	fresh ground black pepper	10 mL
2	cloves crushed garlic	
1 tsp	cayenne powder	
$1/4$ cup	fresh lemon juice (not bottled)	60 mL
	small wooden skewers	

METHOD:

1. Cut chicken or pork into cubes and place in a large bowl. Add olive oil, oregano flakes, salt (optional), black pepper, crushed garlic, cayenne powder and lemon juice. Thoroughly combine all ingredients making sure that the meat cubes are completely coated. Cover the bowl tightly with plastic wrap and refrigerate overnight.

2. Arrange cubes of meat on small wooden skewers. Ensure that the cubes are touching and slightly crowded together.

3. Barbecue kebabs, turning occasionally until cooked. Grilling or broiling method may also be used, however barbecuing produces the authentic flavor.

4. Serve immediately as delicious canapés with cool tzatziki for dipping. Cayenne powder may be left out if a less spicy flavor is preferred.

EXOTIC CAVIAR DIP, P. 3

BELOW:

TANGY STUFFED GRAPE
LEAVES WITH FRESH GROUND
LAMB AND WHITE RICE, P. 114

ASSORTED FRUIT AND FETA CHEESE

BELOW:
SPINACH AND FETA STUFFED PHYLLO P. 21

Tangy Spinach and Toasted Pine Nut Cocktail Crescents

Basic pita dough recipe double quantity

1 1/2 lb	chopped fresh spinach	700 grams
1 1/2 cups	finely chopped green onions	375 mL
1 1/4 tsp	salt (optional)	7 mL
1 tbsp	fresh ground allspice powder	15 mL
1 tsp	fresh ground cinnamon powder	5 mL
1/4 cup	chopped, toasted pine nuts	60 mL
1/4 cup	extra virgin olive oil	60 mL
1/4 cup	fresh squeezed lemon juice	
1	egg, well beaten	
2 tbsp	cold milk, mixed with beaten egg for basting 30 mL	

Method:

1. Wash and chop fresh spinach in small pieces. Place in a large bowl and add chopped onions, salt (optional), spices, olive oil and lemon Juice. Toss all ingredients together and taste. Add toasted pine seeds (pan toasted in 1 tsp butter until golden brown). Mixture should have a distinct lemony flavor.

2. Prepare basic pita dough recipe (doubled quantity). Divide into equal portions about the size of a lemon. On a floured board, roll each of these portions out to a circle shape approximately 3 1/2 inches or 10 cm. in diameter. Place about 2 tbsp or 30 mL of spinach mixture in the center of the circle. Flip pastry over to create a turnover or half-circle shape. Seal edges carefully with the edge of a fork to ensue they are well sealed. Continue this procedure until all the dough and all the spinach mixture is used.

3. Arrange half circles or crescent shapes on a greased, non stick baking dish and brush with egg wash and milk to ensure even browning. Bake at 350° F or 175° C for approximately 15 - 20 minutes or until a light golden color.

4. Remove from oven and cool before serving. These crescents may be made smaller if preferred. Different and delicious!

MINCED SHRIMP AND RED PEPPER PHYLLO APPETIZERS

24	medium sized fresh peeled, cooked shrimp,	
	chopped very finely or coarsely puréed in a food processor	
2	cloves crushed garlic	
1/4 cup	very finely chopped fresh shallots or green onions	60 mL
1/2 cup	very finely chopped sweet red bell peppers	125 mL
2 tbsp	melted butter	30 mL
2 tbsp	fresh parsley, finely chopped	30 mL
1 tbsp	salt (optional)	5 mL
1	package phyllo dough, prepared according to recipe for triangle shapes	
	melted butter for basting	
1 cup	home-made fresh dill mayonnaise	250 mL

METHOD:

1. In a large bowl, place chopped fresh shrimp. Sauté chopped peppers, chopped shallots or green onions in butter just until slightly softened (approximately 3 minutes). Cool and add to shrimp. Add chopped parsley and salt (optional). Add crushed garlic. Combine all ingredients well.

2. Prepare phyllo dough in 2 - 2 1/2 inch or 5 - 6 cm. wide strips, using two sheet thickness. Place a heaping tsp or 5-8 mL of filling at the bottom of the strip and proceed to fold the bottom corner to the opposite edges forming a triangle shape. Continue this process until all filling and phyllo strips are used. Place triangles on a greased baking pan and brush tops evenly with melted butter. Cover with a clean tea towel and allow to sit for about 20 minutes before baking. Bake at 350° F or 175° C for approximately 15 minutes or until golden brown. Remove from heat and serve warm or cool.

3. These canapés are delicious when accompanied by cold, home-made dill mayonnaise for dipping.

MINI GROUND SIRLOIN KEBABS WITH TOASTED PINE NUTS

2 lb	ground top sirloin	1 kg
1 ¼ cup	finely chopped white onion	375 mL
1 ¼ cup	finely chopped parsley	375 mL
2 tsp	fresh ground allspice powder	10 mL
2 tsp	fresh ground cinnamon powder	10 mL
2 tsp	fresh ground black pepper	10 mL
1 tsp	salt (optional)	5 mL
¼ cup	chopped, toasted pine nuts (pan toasted in 2 tbsp or 30 mL butter)	60 mL
	small wooden skewers	

METHOD:

1. Place ground sirloin and spices in a large bowl. In the food processor, combine parsley and onion and chop very finely, almost to a purée consistency. Add toasted pine nuts to parsley and onion and process for an additional ten seconds or so. Add mixture to meat and spices.

2. Combine all ingredients until very well blended. Take enough of the mixture in your hand (about the size of a lime). Press meat mixture against the skewer and squeeze it around the skewer to form a tube shape. Continue to squeeze the meat against the skewer creating irregular grooves. Kebabs should be an irregular shape. If necessary, wet your hand with cold water to prevent sticking.

3. Barbecue the kebabs, turning constantly until the juices of the meat run clear. Grilling and broiling methods may also be used however, barbecuing produces the desired flavor.

4. Serve hot off the grill with either a hummus, eggplant or tzatziki dip. Yum!

SALADS

SIMPLY GREEK VILLAGE SALAD

2	large, ripe and firm red tomatoes (cut in wedges or large chunks)	
1	fresh, firm partly peeled cucumber (English cucumber works well)	
1	medium-size red onion, peeled and cut into thin rings	
$^1/_2$ cup	whole, calamata olives (pits in)	125 mL
1 cup	very coarsely crumbled feta cheese	250 mL
2 tbsp	dry oregano flakes ($^1/_4$ cup or 60 mL fresh oregano leaves may be substituted)	30 mL
$^1/_4$ cup	extra virgin olive oil (more oil may be used if desired)	60 mL
2 tsp	fresh squeezed lemon juice (not bottled). (More lemon juice may be used if desired)	30 mL
	salt to taste	

METHOD:

1. Cut tomatoes into large chunks or wedges, (not slices). Partially peel a cucumber, creating a striped design. Slice the cucumber into approximately 1 inch or 3 cm. slices. Keep the cucumber in circular shapes. Peel and slice the onion.

2. Randomly place all the vegetables in a decorative wide, shallow serving bowl. Add oregano. Toss once. Garnish with olives. Drizzle with olive oil and lemon juice, crumble the feta cheese over the vegetables and finish off by sprinkling a small amount of oregano over the feta. Do not toss after addong the feta cheese.

3. This salad makes a gorgeous centerpiece for a buffet table or great as a main dish or as an accompaniment to any meal.

CHICK-PEA AND KIDNEY BEAN SALAD WITH FRESH TOMATO WEDGES

1 1/2 cups	cooked and drained chick-peas	350 mL
1 1/2 cups	cooked and drained kidney beans	350 mL
2	large, ripe tomatoes, cut in wedges	
1/2 cup	sweet, green bell pepper, cut in strips	125 mL
1/2 cup	sweet, red bell pepper cut in strips	125 mL
1/2 cup	chopped green onions	125 mL
3 cloves	crushed garlic	
1 tsp	salt (optional)	5 mL
1 tsp	fresh ground black pepper	5 mL
1/4 cup	fresh, finely chopped oregano (1 tbsp or 30 mL dry oregano flakes may be substituted)	60 mL
1/4 cup	extra virgin olive oil	
2 tbsp	fresh squeezed lemon juice (not bottled)	30 mL
	curly lettuce for presentation	

METHOD:

1. Combine chick-peas and kidney beans in a large bowl. Add tomato wedges, green and red peppers and chopped green onions. Add crushed garlic, salt (optional), black pepper, oregano, olive oil and lemon juice. Gently toss.

2. Arrange carefully on your choice of decorative, curly lettuce leaves which have been carefully washed and dried. Serve with mini pita bread pockets which may be filled with salad or with crusty fresh Greek bread slices.

3. A wonderful accompaniment to any meal or delicious when served as a main dish.

SWISS CHARD AND RED ONION RING SALAD

4 cups	fresh swiss chard leaves, chopped coarsely	1 litre
1	large red onion, peeled and diced thinly	
2	large ripe but firm tomatoes, cut into large chunks or wedges.	
1	medium-size young cucumber or $^1/2$ English cucumber cut into chunks or slices	
2 cloves	crushed garlic	
1 tsp	salt (optional)	5 mL
$^1/4$ cup	extra virgin olive oil, more may be used if preferred	60 mL
3 tbsp	fresh squeezed lemon juice (not bottled), more may be used if preferred	45 mL
	fresh ground black pepper to taste	

METHOD:

1. Wash swiss chard leaves thoroughly and dry completely. Chop or hand tear into lap pieces and place in a salad bowl. Add sliced onions and tomatoes. Partially peel cucumber to create a striped effect. Add sliced cucumbers to salad. Add the remainder of the ingredients and gently toss until all the vegetables are combined.

2. Place in a decorative salad bowl and serve with any meal. Serve as a main dish with fresh pita bread or fresh crusty Greek bread.

MACARONI ROTINI SALAD WITH MARINATED CHICKEN BREAST

4 cups	cooked, drained and cooled rotini macaroni	1 litre
2	chicken breasts, barbecued (marinated overnight in 2 tbsp or 30 mL olive oil, 2 cloves crushed garlic 2 tbsp or 30 mL lemon juice and 2 tsp or 10 mL oregano flakes), $^1/_2$ tsp or $2^1/_2$ mL dry mint	
$^1/_2$ cup	finely chopped sweet red bell pepper	125 mL
$^1/_2$ cup	finely chopped sweet greed bell pepper	125 mL
$^1/_2$ cup	finely chopped green onion	125 mL
2 tsp	dry oregano flakes	10 mL
2 tsp	dry basil	10 mL
1 tsp	fresh ground black pepper	5 mL
1 tsp	sat (Optional)	
2 cloves	crushed garlic	
$^1/_2$ cup	pitted, sliced calamata olives	125 mL
1 cup	finely chopped ripe, firm red tomatoes	250 mL
$^1/_3$ cup	home-made mayonnaise	80 mL
3 tbsp	extra virgin olive oil	45 mL
1 tbsp	fresh lemon juice (not bottled)	15 mL

METHOD:

1. Marinate chicken breasts overnight in olive oil, garlic, lemon, oregano and mint in a covered container Barbecue over medium heat until tender and juices run clear. Remove from heat and cool in refrigerator.

2. In a large bowl, combine cooked rotini macaroni, chopped peppers, chopped green onions, and chopped olives. Add garlic, oregano, basil and black pepper. Add salt (optional). Add mayonnaise, olive oil and lemon juice. Toss gently.

3. Arrange rotini macaroni salad in a decorative shallow salad dish and decorate the top with cooled chicken breast, which have been cut into strips.

4. This dish makes a wonderful meal on its own with served fresh Greek bread or with toasted pita bread.

TRADITIONAL GREEK GARDEN SALAD

1	large head of iceberg lettuce	
2	large, firm red tomatoes	
1	cucumber washed and partially peeled	
2	cloves of garlic, crushed	
2 tsp	dry oregano flakes	10 mL
1/3 cup	extra virgin olive oil	80 mL
3 tbsp	white vinegar	45 mL
	salt to taste	
1/2 cup	calamata olives (pits in)	125 mL
1/2 cup	feta cheese, coarsely crumbled	125 mL

METHOD:

1. Wash and dry iceberg lettuce thoroughly. Chop in very large chunks and place in a salad bowl.

2. Add tomatoes chopped in large pieces (not wedges). Chop cucumber in large, irregular-shaped chunks, not slices. Add oregano flakes and crushed garlic. Add salt (optional). Add olive oil and vinegar and toss gently.

3. Transfer salad to a decorative dish and randomly add olives. Crumble feta over the salad. Do not toss after adding the feta. Sprinkle the top with a few oregano flakes.

4. Serve with fresh bread. A great summer meal!

SAVORY ROASTED PEPPER AND TOMATO SALAD WITH FRESH MINT

5 large	sweet red bell peppers, roasted, cooled and cut into strips or	
10 large	hot green banana peppers, routed, cooled and cut into strips	
3 cups	chopped, ripe tomatoes	750 mL
4 cloves	crushed garlic	
1 tsp	salt (optional)	5 mL
1/2 cup	finely chopped fresh mint leaves	125 mL
3 tbsp	extra virgin olive oil	45 mL
2 tbsp	fresh squeezed lemon juice (not bottled)	30 mL
1/2 cup	crumbled feta cheese	125 mL

METHOD:

1. Roast the peppers by placing them on a cookie sheet in the oven, directly under the broiler Turning frequently, allow the outer skin to turn black on all sides. Remove from the oven and cool to room temperature. If preferred, place the hot peppers in a plastic bag during the cooling process. This may allow the skin to be more easily removed. Peppers may also be roasted by placing them on the barbecue. The most effective method which creates the truly roasted flavor is achieved by placing the raw peppers directly on the electric burner of the stove. Turning frequently and ensuring the heat is not too high will prevent disintegration of the pepper. A moderately high heat will ensure that only the outer skin is blackened.

2. Peel off the outer skin of the peppers, remove the stems and seeds. Peppers are traditionally cut or torn into strips, buy may also be chopped. In a large bowl, combine roasted peppers and tomatoes. Add crushed garlic, salt and fresh mint. Add oil and lemon juice and toss lightly. Arrange on a decorative serving platter and top with crumbled feta cheese. Add lots of fresh crusty Greek bread for dipping.

Note: Roasted peppers are commonly served with Mediterranean meals. Any type of peppers can be roasted and prepared in the traditional method. When served as a condiment, they are usually cut into strips and placed on a plate, on their own. They are drizzled with a combination of crushed garlic, fresh lemon juice and extra virgin olive oil, and garnished with either finely chopped mint or parsley. Allowing them to marinate in the refrigerator for a few hours before serving brings out the flavor. They are often accompanied by feta cheese and calamata olives.

GREEK POTATO SALAD

4 cups	boiled, cooled red or white potatoes, skin not removed	1 litre
1/2 cup	chopped fresh sweet green bell peppers	125 mL
1/2 cup	chopped fresh sweet red bell peppers	125 mL
1/2 cup	finely chopped green onions	125 nil.
2	large cloves crushed garlic	
1/4 tsp	Hungarian paprika	
	salt and pepper to taste	
1/4 cup	calamata olives not canned (Optional)	60 mL
1/4 cup	finely chopped fresh oregano leaves	60 mL
1/4 cup	extra virgin olive oil	125 mL
3 tbsp	fresh lemon juice (not bottled)	45 mL
1	bunch decorative lettuce for presentation	

METHOD:

1. In a large bowl, combine potatoes which have been cooked to tender and cut into small cubes with chopped peppers, green onions, crushed garlic, chopped fresh oregano and salt and pepper. Add oil and lemon juice and toss gently.

2. Arrange on a bed of decorative lettuce and refrigerate for at least 2 – 3 hours. Just before serving, garnish with calamata olives and sprinkle with paprika.

Cool and Crunchy Cucumber and Tomato Summer Salad

2	fresh cucumbers, partially peeled and diced	
4	large, ripe red tomatoes, diced	
1 cup	finely chopped fresh parsley	250 mL
3 cloves	fresh garlic	
1 tsp	salt (optional)	5 mL
1/4 cup	extra virgin olive oil	60 mL
2 tbsp	fresh lemon juice (not bottled)	30 mL
	iceberg lettuce leaves for presentation	

Method:

1. Wash and remove most of the peel from the cucumbers. Peel length-wise to create a striped effect. Dice cucumber into small pieces. Dice tomatoes into pieces the same size as the cucumbers. Place both in a large bowl and add chopped parsley.

2. Add garlic, salt (optional), olive oil and lemon juice. Toss until well blended.

3. Arrange heaping portions into individual iceberg lettuce leaves. The lettuce creates a very attractive presentation for a very cool and crunchy summer salad.

SENSATIONAL FAVA BEAN SALAD

3 cups	cooked, canned fava beans	750 mL
3 cloves	crushed garlic	
3 tbsp	sesame seed purée (tahini)	45 mL
2 tbsp	fresh lemon juice. (not bottled)	30 mL
1 tsp	salt (optional)	5 mL

Topping

2 cups	chopped fresh parsley	500 mL
2 cups	diced fresh ripe tomatoes	500 mL
1/2 cup	finely chopped green onions	125 mL
3 tbsp	extra virgin olive oil	45 mL
2 tbsp	fresh lemon juice (not bottled)	30 mL
	salt and pepper to taste	

METHOD:

1. Place fava beans in a large saucepan and bring to a boil over medium heat, stirring occasionally. Remove from heat and cool slightly.

2. When beans are cooled, using a hand potato masher, slightly mash down the beans so that some (not all) of the beans are mashed. Do not remove the liquid. Add sesame seed purée, crushed garlic, lemon and salt (optional). Mixture will have thickened. Set aside.

3. In a separate bowl, combine parsley, tomatoes and green onions. Toss lightly. Pour fava beans into a shallow, decorative serving bowl. Arrange the fresh vegetables over the beans. Do not mix. Sprinkle with the olive oil and fresh lemon juice. Refrigerate for about 15 minutes before serving. Salt and pepper to taste.

4. Serve with black olives and fresh pita bread.

Mixed Garden Salad with Fresh Mint and Toasted Pita Croutons

2	large, ripe red tomatoes	
3 cups	coarsely chopped romaine lettuce	750 mL
3 cups	coarsely chopped parsley leaves	750 mL
1/2 cup	chopped fresh mint leaves	125 mL
1	cucumber, partially peeled and coarsely chopped	
3 cloves	crushed garlic	
1 tsp	salt (optional)	5 mL
1 tsp	fresh ground black pepper	5 mL
1/2 cup	calamata olives (pits in)	125 mL
1	large pita bread, split and oven toasted	
1/3 cup	extra virgin olive oil	80 mL
1/4 cup	lemon juice (not bottled)	60 mL

Method:

1. Separate pita bread layers so that you have two single layers. Tear bread into irregular shaped bite-size pieces and spread evenly over an ungreased non-stick cookie sheet. Toast in a moderate oven until the bread is deep golden brown in color. Remove from heat and cool.

2. In a large bowl, combine chopped tomatoes, lettuce, parsley and mint. Add cucumber. Add crushed garlic, salt (optional), oil and lemon juice. Add black olives and toss thoroughly. All ingredients should be very cool, not room temperature. Just before serving, add pita bread pieces and toss again.

3. Arrange in an attractive salad bowl, such as a deep wooden salad bowl. Looks beautiful and tastes fresh and crunchy.

Delicious Crab and Shrimp Salad with Carrots and Green Peas

2 cups	cooked crab meat, coarsely shredded	500 mL
2 cups	cooked, peeled small shrimp	500 mL
2 cups	frozen baby green peas	500 mL
1 cup	frozen diced carrots	250 mL
1/4 cup	finely chopped fresh celery hearts	60 mL
1/3 cup	home-made mayonnaise	80 mL
1 tbsp	finely grated white onion	15 mL
1 tbsp	fresh lemon juice (not bottled)	15 mL
	salt and pepper to taste	
	romaine or curly lettuce for presentation	
	lemon slices or wedges for garnish	

Method:

1. In a large bowl, combine crab meat, shrimp and green peas. Add diced carrots and celery. Add grated onion, mayonnaise and lemon juice. Toss well until completely blended. Taste and add more mayonnaise if desired. Add salt and pepper to taste.

2. Wash and dry lettuce thoroughly, place decoratively on a round serving platter. Pour the salad mixture in the center of the leaves allowing lettuce around the edges to frame the salad. Garnish with lemon slices or wedges.

SIMPLY GREEK VILLAGE SALAD, P. 34

HOMEMADE SAVORY CHEDDAR,
EGG AND ONION PITAS, P. 26

BELOW:
CLASSIC THREE BEAN SOUP, P. 64

COLORFUL CABBAGE AND CARROT SLAW

2 cups	shredded white cabbage	500 mL
2 cups	shredded red cabbage	500 mL
2 cups	shredded fresh carrots	500 mL
1 clove	crushed garlic	
1/3 cup	home-made mayonnaise	60 mL
2 tbsp	extra virgin olive oil	30 mL
2 tbsp	white vinegar	30 mL
1 tsp	granulated sugar	5 mL
1 tsp	dry oregano flakes	5 mL

METHOD:

1. In a large bowl, combine cabbage and carrots. Add garlic, mayonnaise, olive oil, vinegar, sugar. Add oregano flakes and salt and pepper to taste.

2. Toss well until all ingredients are totally combined. Taste and add more oil or vinegar if desired.

3. A fresh and delicious salad to accompany any meal.

FANTASTIC AND FRESH TABOULI

4 cups	fresh finely chopped parsley loaves	1 litre
2 cups	finely chopped green onions	500 mL
1/2 cup	fresh mint leaves, finely chopped	125 mL
4 cups	finely chopped ripe tomatoes	1 litre
1/3 cup	cracked wheat (bulgur)	80 mL
1/3 cup	extra virgin olive oil	80 mL
1/3 cup	fresh lemon juice, (not bottled)	80 mL
	salt and pepper to taste, romaine lettuce for presentation	

METHOD:

1. Wash parsley, green onions and fresh mint thoroughly and spin dry. Try to use as much of the parsley and mint leaves as possible, discarding the stems. The parsley and the mint may be chopped in a food processor, using the pulse switch, to achieve fine chopping results. The green onions may be chopped by the food processor as well, however the pieces of onion should be larger than the pieces of parsley and mint. The reason for this is that if the onions are too finely chopped, they will become mushy. This should be avoided. All the vegetables should be separate and fluffy after chopping. The tomatoes should be chopped by hand; if a food processor were to be used for them, they would just become too watery.

2. Place cracked wheat (bulgur) in warm water. Stir to remove impurities and discard the cloudy water. Add enough clean, warm water to cover the bulgur and allow it to sit for about a 1/2 hour or until the cracked wheat has absorbed most of the water and has become very soft and fluffy.

3. In a large bowl, combine the parsley, mint and green onions. Add the chopped tomatoes. Squeeze the cracked wheat by hand, making certain that all of the water is removed. Add about a 1/2 cup or 125 mL of the softened, squeezed dry cracked wheat to the salad. Add the olive oil and lemon juice. Add salt and pepper to taste. Taste the salad and add more olive oil or lemon juice if desired.

4. Arrange washed romaine lettuce on a large platter with the stems facing inward. This will create a sun burst pattern. Pour the tabouli in the center of the lettuce. Romaine lettuce leaves may be used as a scoop to pick up the salad. It is best eaten in this fashion. Tabouli looks almost as good as it tastes!

RED BEET SALAD WITH ONION RINGS AND FRESH OREGANO

4 cups	cooked red beets, sliced	1 litre
2 cups	white or red onions, peeled and sliced thinly	500 mL
1/4 cup	fresh chopped oregano leaves	60 mL
1/4 cup	olive oil	60 mL
3 tbsp	white vinegar	45 mL
	salt and pepper to taste	

METHOD:

Combine sliced beets and onion rings in a large bowl. Add chopped oregano leaves. Add olive oil and vinegar. Add salt and pepper to taste. Refrigerate for at least three hours before serving. Serve cold.

STEAMED BROCCOLI AND SAUTÉED RED ONION SALAD

2 bunches	fresh broccoli, cut into pieces	
1 1/2 cups	red onions, slivered	325 mL
1 tbsp	olive oil	1-5 mL
2 cloves	crushed garlic	
1/4 cup	fresh lemon juice, (not bottled)	60 mL
1/4 cup	olive oil	60 mL
	salt and pepper to taste	

METHOD:

1. Wash broccoli thoroughly and cut into pieces. Steam just until barely tender. Do not overcook. Remove from heat and transfer into a large bowl to cool.

2. In a saucepan containing 1 tbsp or 15 mL olive oil, add slivered red onions. Sauté over medium heat until onions begin to caramelize around the edges. Remove from heat and cool.

3. Add cooled onions to cooled broccoli. Add crushed garlic and drizzle with lemon juice and olive oil. Toss gently. Add salt and pepper to taste.

4. This dish is great as a salad or as a vegetable accompaniment to any meal.

TANGY SUMMER TOMATO AND ONION RING SALAD

3 cups	large, ripe tomatoes cut into wedges or chunks	750 mL
2 cups	white onions, sliced thinly	500 mL
1/4 cup	chopped fresh oregano leaves	60 mL
1/4 cup	extra virgin olive oil	60 mL
3 tbsp	white vinegar	45 mL
	salt and pepper to taste	

METHOD:

Combine tomatoes and onion rings in a large bowl. Add chopped oregano leaves, olive oil and lemon juice. Add salt and pepper to taste. Toss gently and refrigerate for about three hours before serving. Serve cold.

LENTIL SALAD WITH FRESH VEGETABLES

¹/₂ cup	chopped sweet, red bell peppers	125 mL
¹/₂ cup	chopped sweet, green bell peppers	125 mL
¹/₂ cup	chopped sweet, yellow bell peppers	125 mL
¹/₂ cup	chopped celery hearts	125 mL
¹/₂ cup	chopped green onions	125 mL
³/₄ cup	chopped red tomatoes	180 mL
¹/₄ cup	chopped fresh parsley	60 mL
2 cups	cooked and drained lentils	500 mL
2 clove	crushed garlic	
¹/₄ cup	extra virgin olive oil	60 mL
3 tbsp	fresh lemon juice, (not bottled)	45 mL
	salt and pepper to taste	
	iceberg lettuce for presentation	

METHOD:

1. Wash and chop peppers, celery and green onions and place them in a large bowl. Add chopped parsley, cooked lentils, chopped tomatoes and crushed garlic. Add oil, lemon and salt and pepper to taste. Toss lightly until all ingredients are well blended.

2. Wash and separate iceberg lettuce leaves. Place heaping spoons of salad into each iceberg lettuce leaf when serving. This is a very attractive salad as well as being very refreshing to the taste. It may easily be served as a main dish.

TANGY SWISS CHARD AND RISOTTO SALAD

2 cups	risotto cooked in boiling salted water	500 mL
4 cups	fresh Swiss chard (not frozen)	1 litre
2 cups	chopped ripe tomatoes	500 mL
1/2 cup	finely chopped green onions	125 mL
1/4 cup	finely chopped fresh parsley leaves	60 mL
3 cloves	crushed garlic	
1 tsp	salt (optional)	5 mL
1 tsp	fresh ground black pepper	
1/2 tsp	crushed chili pepper flakes and seeds (optional)	2.5 mL
1/4 cup	extra virgin olive oil	60 mL
3 tbsp	fresh lemon juice (not bottled)	45 mL

METHOD:

1. Cook risotto in boiling water until very tender and fluffy. Remove from heat, rinse in cold water, drain and cool.

2. Thoroughly wash fresh Swiss chard and chop finely. Steam Swiss chard for approximately 3 minutes or just until softened. Remove from heat, drain and cool.

3 In a large bowl, place cooled risotto. Add the drained Swiss chard. Squeeze Swiss chard by hand removing all of the excess water and add to the risotto. Add chopped tomatoes and green onions. Add the remainder of ingredients and toss carefully, taking care not to mash the risotto.

4. This dish may be served warm or cold and may be garnished with black olives or feta cheese. Spinach may be used in place of Swiss chard if desired. A delicious addition to any meal or perfect on its own.

EGGS AND OMELETS

EGGS AND OMELETS

Traditional Greek omelets are made from a number of combinations of ingredients. There are vegetarian combinations as well as omelets containing both meat and vegetables. They are cooked in either butter or olive oil, depending on one's preference but whichever combination is chosen, any one of the traditional Greek omelets is quick and easy and always a delicious taste experience. The omelet recipes to follow are proportioned in each case to serve two.

FRESH TOMATO OMELET

5	large eggs, beaten until light and fluffy	
2 tbsp	milk	30 mL
1 cup	chopped fresh ripe tomatoes	250 mL
1 clove	crushed garlic	
2 tbsp	melted butter or olive oil	30 mL
$1/2$ tsp	fresh ground black pepper	3 mL
	salt to taste	
$1/4$ cup	crumbled feta cheese (optional)	60 mL

METHOD:

1. In a non-stick pan containing olive oil, sauté garlic for approximately 30 seconds. Add chopped fresh tomato, salt and pepper. Sauté over medium heat until tomatoes become soft and melted, about 3 minutes.

2. In a small bowl, beat eggs until fluffy. Add milk and continue to beat for about a half a minute. Add the egg mixture to the pan containing tomatoes. Cook over medium beat, pushing the mixture from the sides toward the middle gently with a wooden spatula until the eggs begin to get fluffy. Feta cheese may be crumbled over the top at this point, if desired. Cover the eggs and reduce heat to low. Allow to cook until the cheese begins to melt. Serve immediately.

SAVORY POTATO AND EGG OMELET

2 cups	raw potatoes, peeled and finely diced	500 mL
1 tsp	Hungarian paprika	5 mL
1 tsp	garlic powder or 1 clove crushed garlic	5 mL
2 tbsp	melted butter or olive oil	30 mL
1/2 tsp	fresh ground black pepper	3 mL
5	large eggs, beaten until light and fluffy	
2 tbsp	milk	
1/2 tsp	salt (optional)	

METHOD:

1. In a non-stick skillet containing butter or olive oil, add paprika and diced pota-toes. Sauté over medium heat, turning often, until potatoes begin to turn golden brown. Add crushed garlic or garlic powder at this stage.

2. In a small bowl, combine eggs and milk. Beat until light and foamy. Add salt and pepper. Pour egg mixture into hot pan containing cooked potatoes. Stir constantly from sides of the pan toward the middle until eggs are fluffy. Serve immediately.

Fresh Leek and Feta Cheese Omelet

1/2 cup	fresh leeks, finely chopped (white part only)	125 mL
1/2 cup	crumbled feta cheese	125 mL
2 tbsp	melted butter or olive oil	30 mL
5	eggs, well beaten	
2 tbsp	milk	30 mL
1/2 tsp	salt (optional)	3 mL
	pepper to taste	

Method:

1. In a non-stick pan containing olive oil or melted butter, add chopped leeks and sauté until soft and slightly golden brown in color.

2. In a bowl, combine eggs and milk and beat until light and fluffy. Add salt and pepper to taste. Add egg mixture to the hot pan containing cooked leeks and stir constantly from sides toward center of the pan. This motion creates fluffiness. When the eggs are half or almost cooked, add the crumbled feta cheese. Cover the pan and reduce heat until the eggs are done and the cheese is melted. Serve immediately.

FRESH SPINACH OR SWISS CHARD OMELET WITH FETA CHEESE

2 cups	fresh, finely chopped spinach or Swiss chard	500 mL
2 tbsp	finely chopped green onion	30 mL
2 tbsp	melted butter or olive oil	30 mL
5	eggs, well beaten	
2 tbsp	milk	30 mL
1/4 cup	crumbled feta cheese (optional)	60 mL
	salt and pepper to taste	

METHOD:

1. Wash and finely chop the spinach or Swiss chard. Sauté in a non-stick pan containing melted butter or olive oil, together with chopped onions until both spinach/Swiss chard and onions are soft and onions are beginning to turn golden brown around the edges.

2. In a small bowl, combine eggs and milk and beat until light and foamy. Add egg mixture to the hot pan containing vegetables. Cook over medium heat stirring from sides to center of the pan until eggs are almost cooked and fluffy. This is the time to crumble the feta cheese over the top if desired. Cover and reduce the heat until the eggs are cooked and the feta cheese is melted. Serve immediately.

SPICY BACON, TOMATO AND HOT PEPPER OMELET WITH MELTED FETA CHEESE

1/2 lb	bacon cut into small pieces and fried crisp	225 grams
1 cup	finely chopped flesh ripe tomatoes	250 mL
1/4 cup	hot banana peppers, chopped finely, seeds and stem removed.	60 mL
2 cloves	crushed garlic	
2 tbsp	melted butter or olive oil	30 mL
5	eggs, well beaten	
2 tbsp	milk	30 mL
1/4 cup	crumbled feta cheese	60 mL
	salt and pepper to taste	

METHOD:

1. Cut bacon into small pieces and fry until crisp. Remove from heat and drain thoroughly on a paper towel to remove all excess fat.

2. In a non-stick pan containing melted butter or olive oil, add chopped hot banana peppers. If using hot banana peppers, the omelet will be very hot and spicy. Sweet green or red or yellow peppers may be substituted, if desired. Add crushed garlic. Sauté over medium heat until peppers begin to turn light golden brown. Add drained bacon pieces and chopped tomatoes. Combine all ingredients well.

3. In a small bowl, combine eggs and milk and beat until light and foamy. Add salt and pepper to taste. Pour the egg mixture into the hot pan containing bacon and vegetables. Cook over medium heat, stirring from sides toward center until the eggs are almost cooked and fluffy. This is the time to add the feta cheese, if desired. Cover the pan and reduce the heat until the eggs are cooked and the feta cheese is melted. Serve immediately. Spicy and delicious!

FRESH DILL WEED AND FETA CHEESE OMELET

5	eggs, well beaten	
2 tbsp	milk	30 mL
2 tbsp	chopped fresh dill weed	30 mL
1/4 cup	crumbled feta cheese	60 mL
	salt and pepper to taste	
2 tbsp	melted butter or olive oil	30 mL

METHOD:

1. In a non-stick pan, add chopped dill weed to melted butter or olive oil. Just heat for approximately 30 seconds.

2. In a small bowl, combine eggs and milk and beat until light and foamy. Add salt and pepper to taste. Add the egg mixture to the hot pan containing the chopped dill weed. Cook over medium heat, stirring constantly from sides toward the center of the pan until eggs are almost cooked. Add feta cheese, if desired, and cover the pan and reduce the heat until the eggs are cooked and the feta cheese is melted.

POACHED EGGS WITH PAPRIKA AND MELTED BUTTER SAUCE

4	eggs, poached	
4 tbsp	melted butter	60 mL
1 1/2 tsp	Hungarian paprika	8 mL
	salt and pepper to taste	
4 tbsp	cold water	60 mL
4	slices of toast	

METHOD:

1. Poach eggs in an egg poacher or in salted water. Eggs may be cooked soft or medium. Place the cooked eggs on four slices of dry toast.

2. In a saucepan, melt butter and add paprika. Add salt and pepper. Allow the butter to begin to sizzle and immediately add the cold water. Let this mixture come to a boil and immediately pour over the eggs. Serve immediately. Eggs may be accompanied by crisp bacon slices or any type of breakfast sausage, or eaten on their own. Different and tasty!

   Pan fried eggs, over-easy may be substituted for poached eggs in this recipe.

SOUPS

HEARTY CHICKEN VEGETABLE SOUP

1 - 2 ^{1}/2 lb whole chicken, cut into pieces		1 kg
1 cup	coarsely chopped celery hearts	250 mL
1 cup	coarsely chopped white onions	250 mL
1 cup	coarsely chopped carrots	250 mL
2 cups	coarsely chopped white potatoes	500 mL
^{1}/2 cup	uncooked rice	125 mL
2 cloves	crushed garlic	
1 tbsp	butter	
1 tsp	fresh ground black pepper	5 mL
1 tsp	salt (optional)	5 mL
2 tbsp	fresh lemon juice (not bottled)	30 mL
8 cups	chicken stock	2 litres

METHOD:

1. Wash chicken thoroughly and cut into pieces. Removing the skin will lower the fat content of the soup. Place pieces of chicken in a large soup pot, cover with cold water and bring them to a boil. When the chicken pieces come to a full boil, a foamy substance will form. Discard all of the water and the foam. Rinse the chicken with cold water and discard the water. Cover the chicken pieces with approximately 8 cups or 2 litres of chicken stock. Cover and simmer over moderate heat until the chicken is completely cooked. When the chicken is fully cooked, it will be separating from the bones and the liquid in the pot will have reduced to about half of the original amount. Set aside to cool.

2. When the chicken has cooled, remove the pieces from the pot one at a time and remove the meat from the bones by hand. Discard all of the bones, leaving the chicken meat in large pieces. Place deboned chicken in a separate dish and place in the refrigerator until ready to use. Retain the stock.

3. Using a large sieve, strain the chicken stock into a clean soup pot. There should be about 1 litre of liquid left over from the boiling process. Add an additional litre of chicken or vegetable stock or water to the existing stock to make approximately 2 litres. Add chopped garlic, chopped onions, celery and carrots. Bring this mixture to a boil and reduce heat. Simmer over medium heat until the carrots and celery begin to soften, approximately 15 minutes. Wash and drain the uncooked rice and potatoes to the vegetables. Add the cooked chicken pieces. Cover and simmer for an additional 15 minutes over medium heat until rice is fluffy and vegetables are tender. Stir only once or twice. Excessive stirring will make the soup mushy. Just before serving, add butter and fresh lemon juice. Enjoy piping hot as a main dish with fresh, crusty Greek bread.

CLASSIC THREE BEAN SOUP
(SERVED HOT OR COLD)

1 cup	canned lima beans in liquid	250 mL
1 cup	canned navy beans in liquid	250 mL
1 cup	canned red kidney beans in liquid	250 mL
1/2 cup	finely chopped sweet red bell pepper	125 mL
1/2 cup	finely chopped sweet green bell pepper	125 mL
1/2 cup	finely chopped celery	125 mL
1/2 cup	finely chopped white onion	125 mL
2 tsp	Hungarian paprika	10 mL
2 tsp	fresh ground black pepper	10 mL
2 tsp	dry oregano flakes	10 mL
2 cloves	crushed garlic	
1 tsp	salt (optional)	5 mL
1 1/2 cups	finely chopped or puréed stewed tomatoes	375 mL
4 tbsp	extra virgin olive oil	60 mL
1 cup	water or beef or vegetable stock	250 mL

METHOD:

1. In a large soup pot containing olive oil, add chopped peppers, celery and onions. Add paprika, black pepper, crushed garlic and oregano flakes. Sauté over medium heat until onions become transparent.

2. Add the beans and their liquid to the sautéed vegetables. Add the stewed tomatoes and water or beef or vegetable stock. Stir well until all ingredients are combined. Cover and simmer over low heat for about 1/2 hour until the flavors are blended. Add salt to taste.

3. This soup may be served as an appetizer, as a side dish or even as a main dish. It may be eaten cold as well as hot. With pita bread and a salad it makes a hearty and delicious meatless meal.

Traditional Greek Chicken Soup

12 - 1/2 lb	fresh whole chicken	
8 cups	chicken stock or water	2 litres
1 cup	finely chopped white onion	250 mL
1 clove	crushed garlic	
1 tsp	salt (optional)	5 mL
1 tsp	fresh ground block pepper	5 mL
2 cups	broad noodles	500 mL
	or	
1 cup	uncooked rice	250 mL
3 tbsp	fresh lemon juice (not bottled)	45 mL

Method:

1. Wash and cut fresh chicken into pieces. Add cold water and bring to a boil. Discard the water when it boils and forms a foamy film. Wash the chicken and add the stock. Cover and allow the chicken to simmer over medium heat for approximately 1 1/2 hours or until the chicken is separating from the bones. Remove from heat and cool.

2. Remove the cooled chicken from the stock and separate the chicken meat from the bones. Discard all of the bones and the skin. Pour the remaining chicken stock through a sieve into a clean soup pot. Add enough water or additional chicken stock to make about 2 litres or 8 cups of liquid. Add the chopped onion, crushed garlic and the noodles or rice.

3. Cover and simmer over medium heat for about a 1/2 hour. Add the chicken pieces and the fresh lemon juice. Add salt and pepper to taste. Simmer for an additional 15 minutes and serve piping hot.

RICH AND DELICIOUS BEEF BARLEY SOUP

1 ¹/2 lb	stewing beef	650 grams
1	large beef soup bone with marrow	
¹/2 cup	chopped white onion	125 mL
¹/2 cup	chopped carrots	125 mL
¹/2 cup	chopped celery hearts	125 mL
1 ¹/2 cup	chopped white potatoes	375 mL
³/4 cup	uncooked barley	180 mL
8 cups	water or beef stock	2 litres
1 tsp	fresh ground black pepper	5 mL
1 tsp	salt (optional)	5 mL
¹/2 tsp	fresh ground allspice powder	3 mL
1 clove	crushed garlic	

METHOD:

1. Wash and cut beef into small pieces and place in a large soup pot. Wash a large beef soup bone with marrow and place in the soup pot with the meat. Cover with cold water and bring to a boil. When the water comes to a boil, it will become cloudy and foamy. Discard this water. Cover the beef and soup bone with fresh cold water. For a richer taste, use beef stock or vegetable stock. Cover and simmer over medium heat for approximately 2 hours or until the meat is very tender and soft. The water will have reduced to less than half of the original amount. At this point the soup bone can be removed and discarded. The marrow inside the bone is traditionally retained and used as an ingredient of the soup, but it may be discarded, if preferred. It does however, add flavor and nutritional value to the stock while cooking.

2. Remove the meat and place it in a clean soup pot. Strain the remaining stock through a sieve into the pot. Add additional water or stock to make up about 2 litres or 8 cups of liquid. Add the crushed garlic and all of the vegetables except the potatoes. Cover and simmer for about 15 minutes over medium heat until the carrots just begin to soften. Reduce heat and add the barley and the pota-

toes. Cover and simmer for an additional 15 minutes or until the potatoes are just tender and the barley is soft and fluffy.

3. For a slightly less thick soup, $1/2$ cup or 125 mL of barley may be used. Serve this delicious soup as a main course with fresh crusty Greek bread.

SAVORY MINI MEATBALL NOODLE SOUP

1 lb	extra lean ground sirloin	450 grams
$1/2$ cup	finely chopped white onion	125 mL
1 clove	crushed garlic	
2 tbsp	olive oil	30 mL
$1/2$ tsp	fresh ground black pepper	3 mL
1 tsp	dry oregano flakes	5 mL
$1/2$ cup	finely chopped carrots	125 mL
$1/2$ cup	finely chopped celery hearts	125 mL
6 cups	beef stock	$1^1/2$ litres
2 cups	uncooked, wide noodles	500 mL
2 tbsp	fresh lemon juice (not bottled)	30 mL

METHOD:

1. Shape ground sirloin into mini meatballs about the size of cherries. Brown the meatballs in olive oil. Add crushed garlic, chopped onion, chopped carrots and chopped celery to cooked meatballs. Add the spices and combine all the ingredients.

2. Add beef stock and bring to a boil. Add uncooked noodles, cover and simmer over low heat for about 15 - 20 minutes or until noodles are soft. Just before serving, add fresh lemon juice.

3. This soup makes a hearty meal when served with crusty Greek bread and any salad.

Tasty Navy Bean and Beef Soup

3 cups	canned navy beans in liquid	750 mL
1 lb	stewing beef	450 grams
3/4 cup	finely chopped white onion	180 mL
1/2 cup	finely chopped carrots	125 mL
1/2 cup	finely chopped celery hearts	125 mL
1/4 cup	finely chopped sweet red bell peppers	60 mL
1/4 cup	finely chopped sweet green bell peppers	60 mL
2 tbsp	extra virgin olive oil	30 mL
1 cup	chopped, stewed tomatoes (may be puréed to eliminate chunks)	250 mL
1 tsp	fresh ground black pepper	5 mL
1 tsp	salt (optional)	
2 tsp	dry oregano flakes	10 mL
1 1/2 tsp	Hungarian paprika	
6 cups	beef or vegetable stock	1 1/2 litres

Method:

1. Wash the beef thoroughly in cold water, cut it into bite-size pieces and simmer in water until it comes to a boil. Discard the water and add about 6 - 8 cups or 2 litres of water or beef or vegetable stock. The beef or vegetable stock will produce a fuller flavor in the soup. Cover the beef and simmer for about 2 hours over medium heat until the meat is very soft and tender. Remove from heat and set aside.

2. In a clean soup pot containing 2 tbsp olive oil, sauté the chopped onions just until they begin to soften. Add the vegetables, tomatoes and spices and combine all ingredients. Add the cooked beans and liquid to the sautéed vegetables. Strain remaining stock through a sieve into the new pot and add the beef pieces. If the soup appears too thick, add additional beef or vegetable stock or water. Add salt and pepper to taste. Cover and simmer for approximately 1/2 hour over low heat until the soup flavors come together. Stir occasionally; soup will thicken as it simmers.

3. A great main dish served with a salad and fresh pita bread!

CREAMY LEEK AND POTATO SOUP

3 cups	fresh leeks, chopped finely	750 mL
3 cups	finely chopped white potatoes	750 mL
4 cups	light chicken stock	1 litre
2 tbsp	butter	30 mL
1 tsp	salt (optional)	5 mL
1 tsp	fresh ground black pepper	5 mL
1 1/2 cups	light cream or whole milk (2% milk may be used for a lighter flavor)	375 mL

METHOD:

1. Thoroughly wash and chop fresh leeks, ensuring to remove all the sand. In a non-stick pan containing melted butter, sauté the leeks over medium heat until they become soft. Do not brown. Remove from the heat and cool. Place the leeks in a food processor just until they are smooth and soft. Do not puré. We want the soup to have texture.

2. Simmer the chopped potatoes in the light chicken broth until they are very soft, even mushy. Add salt and pepper to taste. Add the chopped leeks. Simmer over low heat for about a 1/2 hour, stirring occasionally until the flavors are blended together. Add the cream before serving and stir. The soup will thicken at this point. If preferred, a total creamy texture may be achieved by puréeing the soup with a food processor or an electric hand food processor.

3. This soup has a rich yet delicate flavor.

TRADITIONAL GREEK LENTIL SOUP WITH FRESH LEEKS

2 cups	cooked lentils (canned lentils in liquid may be used)	500 mL
1/3 cup	finely chopped leeks (white part only)	80 mL
1/3 cup	finely chopped celery hearts	80 mL
1/3 cup	finely chopped carrots	80 mL
1 tsp	salt (optional)	5 mL
1 tsp	fresh ground black pepper	5 mL
2 tsp	dry oregano flakes	10 mL
2 tsp	Hungarian paprika	10 mL
2 cloves	crushed garlic	
4 tbsp	extra virgin olive oil	60 mL
1 1/2 cups	stewed tomatoes, puréed	375 mL
3 cups	beef or vegetable stock or water	750 mL

METHOD:

1. Thoroughly wash and chop leeks and sauté in a large soup pot in 4 tbsp olive oil. Add oregano, salt and pepper. Add chopped vegetables and crushed garlic. Add stewed tomatoes and cooked lentils. Finally, add the beef or vegetable stock.

2. Cover and simmer over medium heat, stirring regularly for about a 1/2 hour or until the soup thickens and the flavors blend together.

3. This is a delicious and very traditional Greek soup which is often eaten as a main dish when accompanied by fresh Greek bread and a salad. Don't forget the calamata olives and feta cheese!

BREADS AND DOUGHS

Basic pita dough may be used for a wide variety of recipes. The ingredients remain the same for each recipe, however the quantities may vary slightly. For example, when making the basic pita dough recipe for focaccia, use 2 tbsp or 30 mL of yeast. This extra amount of yeast will make the dough rise higher and will produce a fluffier and more bread-like texture. Any time this fluffier, more bread-like texture is desired, simply add the extra amount of yeast. The basic recipe would be more commonly used for recipes such as Egg and Onion Pitas or for Spinach and Toasted Pine Nut Cocktail Crescents. If one were to use this recipe as an alternative to phyllo dough when preparing tube or strudel type pastry, or for round pie crust, the amount of yeast should be reduced to 2 tsp or 10 mL. The reason for this reduction in yeast amount for these recipes is that when using the pastry as a substitute for phyllo dough, a very bread-like consistency is not desired. The method of preparation will also change according to the way the dough is being used, as explained below under "Method For Tubes, Strudels and Pie Crust. One very important point to remember - no matter what recipe is being prepared using the basic pita dough, always allow the finished prod-uct to stand in the pan to proof for twenty minutes before placing in the oven to bake."

Basic Pita Dough

3 cups	all purpose flour (white or whole wheat)	750 mL
3 tbsp	canola oil	45 mL
1 tsp	salt	5 mL
2 tsp	sugar	10 mL
2 tbsp	traditional dry yeast	30 mL
1 cup	warm water	250 mL
	Additional warm water	

When using pita dough for the purpose of making strudel or tube pastry, or pie crust,

3/4 cup	melted butter	180 mL

is included in the recipe for brushing the pastry.

METHOD FOR PITAS, CRESCENTS OR PIZZA CRUST:

1. In a small bowl containing one cup of warm water, add sugar and sprinkle dry yeast on the top. Briefly stir and allow to sit for about ten minutes or until the yeast begins to bubble and activate.

2. In a large bowl, combine flour and salt. Add oil and the yeast mixture to the flour. Add enough additional warm water to allow the ingredients to blend together. Mixture should not be sticky. If the dough is sticky, add extra flour, gradually, until a soft pliable ball can be formed. The dough should feel very soft. Gently knead the dough for about one minute and shape it into a smooth ball. Cover the dough with a clean towel and allow it to sit at room temperature for about a $1/2$ hour, or until it has almost doubled in size.

3. After the dough has risen, it may be used according to each individual recipe calling for basic pita dough.

BASIC PITA DOUGH —
METHOD FOR TUBES, STRUDELS AND PIE CRUST

1. This method of preparing basic pita dough is the same as the previous one until the dough has been formed into a smooth ball. Use 1 tsp dry yeast only for tubes, strudels and pie crust. At this point, divide the dough into nine equal parts. Roll each of these parts by hand, to form a small ball shape. Place the nine balls on a floured pastry board and cover with a clean towel.

2. Melt 3/4 cup of butter and remove from heat. Using a rolling pin, roll each of the balls out to approximately a 6 in. or 15 cm. diameter circle. Combine them in groups of threes. Roll out the first circle and brush the top with melted butter. Roll out the second circle and place it on top of the previous one. Brush the top with melted butter. Roll out the third circle and place it on the top of the previous one. Do not brush the top of the third circle with melted butter. Set this three-level circle aside and repeat this process with the remaining balls of dough. The result will be three, three-layer circles with melted butter between the layers.

3. Cover the circles with a clean tea towel. Roll the circles out on a floured board, using a rolling pin. The objective is to roll the dough out as thin as possible. The final result will be a circle approximately 24 in. or 60 cm. in diameter. Use any of the fillings suggested in the book for stuffed phyllo. Basic pita dough may be substituted for phyllo dough to create tubes or strudels.

4. To create a top and bottom crust for a pie, combine two of the three final three-layer circles by brushing the surface of one and placing the second on top, making a six-layer circle. Roll this six-layer circle out to at least 24 in. or 60 cm. in

diameter. Place the sheet on a buttered, round 18 in. or 45 cm. diameter pan, an equivalent size rectangular pan may be used. The dough will be too large for the pan. It should be manoeuvred and crowded to fit. It will not have a smooth appearance in the pan. Any of the fillings suggested for the stuffed phyllo recipe may be used. Brush the surface of the crust lightly with melted butter and spread the filling evenly. Roll the remaining triple-layer circle out and manoeuvre it over the filling to create a very wrinkled top crust. If you prefer the pie to have a thicker edge, allow 3/4 in. or 2 cm. to hang over the sides of the pan. Brush with melted butter and twist the dough to create a decorative edge. Brush the surface of the pie with melted butter. Cover with a clean tea towel and allow it to proof at room temperature about a half hour before baking. This assists in the rising process. Bake at 350° F or 175° C for approximately 35 minutes or until the crust is golden brown and the pie has risen. Check the bottom crust occasionally during baking to prevent overcooking. Remove the baked pie from the oven and cover with a clean towel. Allow it to cool slightly before serving.

5. The use of home-made basic pita dough for tubes, strudels and pies is the original and authentic way used by the Greeks for centuries, long before commercial phyllo was available. Phyllo dough, however, is a good and fast alternative. Many Greeks still use the home-made dough, even though it is time-consuming. Try it and you will understand why. Absolutely delicious!

HOME-MADE CRUSTY GREEK BREAD TRADITIONAL METHOD

8 cups	all-purpose flour (white or whole wheat)	2 litres
4 tbsp	traditional dry yeast	60 mL
1 cup	warm water	250 mL
2 tsp	sugar	10 mL
1 tsp	salt	5 mL
2 tbsp	canola oil	60 mL
2 tbsp	melted butter	60 mL
3 cups	warm water	750 mL
2	egg yolks, well beaten	
1/4 cup	milk	60 mL
3 tbsp	sesame seeds (optional)	45 mL

METHOD:

1. Dissolve sugar in one cup of warm water. Add yeast and stir once. Allow to sit at room temperature for about 15 minutes until it foams up and rises.

2. Wash your hands thoroughly, as you will be working with dough. Sift flour into a very large bowl. Make a well in the center of the flour. Add salt, oil, butter and prepared yeast mixture. The blending process is done with one hand only. The other hand is used only to add the ingredients. Add warm water to the center of the mixture. Using your blending hand, gradually incorporate the warm water into the flour and other ingredients, working from the center, outward. Continue adding warm water until all of the flour is incorporated. The dough should not be dry, it should be soft and easy to knead. If it is too dry, add more warm water; if it is too wet, add more flour. Add the sticky dough from you blending hand to the main dough. Wash and dry your hands.

3. Remove the dough from the bowl and place it on a well-floured kneading surface. Flour the top of the dough and begin to knead the dough with both hands, turning regularly, for approximately ten minutes. Sprinkle the dough with additional flour if it becomes sticky. The result should be a smooth soft ball of dough. Place kneaded dough in a large, oiled bowl. Brush the top of the dough with oil to keep it soft while rising. Cover with a clean towel and allow it to rise

until it doubles in size, approximately 1 $1/2$ to 2 hours. Remove dough from the bowl and place it on a floured kneading board. Punch it down and knead it again for about 5 minutes. If a fluffy, more airy bread is desired, make large slashes in the dough during the kneading process, using a sharp knife. This permits the air to enter and creates air pockets. The end result is fluffier, less dense bread. This is a matter of preference. It does not affect the taste or quality of the bread. Place the dough in a very large, oiled bowl. Brush the top of the dough with oil and allow it to rise for an additional $1/2$ to $3/4$ hour.

4. The dough may be baked in many shapes. Loaf shapes are achieved by using loaf pans. The dough may also be separated and made into small, individual rolls. The traditional shape of Greek bread, however, is round. Using a round pan such as an 8 in. or 20 cm. cake pan, separate the dough into four equal parts. Knead each part briefly into a smooth ball and place one ball in the center of each oiled pan. This recipe may also be used to make one large, round loaf. Large, round bread pans are available at specialty Greek grocery stores. They are approximately 16 in. or 40 cm, in diameter and have a depth of 2 in. or 5 cm.

5. When placing the balls of dough in the pans, ensure that all of the creases are tucked in on the bottom. The top surface of the dough should be perfectly round and smooth. Combine egg yolks and milk in a small bowl and beat until fluffy. Brush the tops of the dough(s), after placing them in the pans, thoroughly and evenly with the egg wash. Sprinkle with raw sesame seeds, (optional). The sesame seeds will become toasted during the baking process. Cover with a towel and allow it to rise for one hour before baking.

6. Bake in a preheated oven at 350° F or 175° C for approximately 15 minutes. Reduce the heat to 300° F or 150° C and continue baking for approximately 35 minutes, depending on the size of the loaf. A larger loaf will, of course need more baking time. The bread is done when it is an even golden brown color.

7. Remove the bread from the oven and cool at room temperature before removing it from the pan. The bread should be completely cooled before slicing. The cooling time should be at least four hours. Superb with everything, and delicious on its own!

TRADITIONAL EASTER BREAD
(SWEET EGG LOAF)

Best to read the recipe before starting

10 cups	all purpose white flour (about 3 $^1/_2$ lb)	2 $^1/_2$ litres
2 cups	milk	500 mL
2 cups	sugar	500 mL
1 tbsp	lemon rind	15 mL
$^1/_2$ lb	melted butter	225 mL
4 tsp	sugar	20 mL
2 cups	warm water	500 mL
4 tbsp	traditional dry yeast	60 mL
6	eggs, well beaten	
2 cups	flour for kneading	500 mL
2	egg yolks, well beaten	
4 tbsp	sesame seeds	60 mL

(Thoroughly wash and dry hands before beginning)

METHOD:

1. Preheat oven to 200° F or 90° C and shut it off. Measure the flour in a large shallow pan, forming a mound shape with a hole in the center.

2. Combine 2 cups of sugar and 2 cups of milk and beat until sugar has completely dissolved. Add lemon. Find and melted butter and cool. Add yeast to 2 cups of warm water containing 4 tsp sugar and stir. Allow yeast to sit at room temperature for 15 minutes until it begins to rise. Beat 6 eggs with an electric beater for about 3 minutes, add to the cooled milk mixture and stir.

3. The stirring process of the flour is done by hand, using one hand only to stir and the other hand to add the ingredients. Begin to mix the dough by pouring $^1/_2$ of the milk and egg mixture into the center of the flour. Using one hand to stir, bring the flour from all sides toward the center. Continue to add the remaining milk and egg mixture, gradually. Stir the prepared yeast and add to the dough. Incorporate all of the flour into the liquid ingredients, keeping the dough soft. If the dough is too dry add warm water in small amounts. If the dough is too wet add additional flour in small amounts. Remove the particles

from your mixing hand and add to the dough. The dough should be very soft and pliable but not sticky. Wash and dry hands thoroughly. Place the dough on a heavily floured board and knead with both hands for about 10 minutes. During the kneading process, cut slashes in the dough with a sharp knife, often. This allows air to enter the dough and creates a fluffy, airy loaf. Add more flour as needed to keep the dough from sticking. Continue kneading and slashing for an additional 5 minutes. The total kneading time should be 15 minutes.

4. Place the dough in the center of a large, 18 in. or 45 cm. well-buttered pan. Ensure that all of the creases and lines of the dough are on the bottom. The top of the dough should appear perfectly smooth and round. Brush the dough on all sides with melted butter. This will prevent a crust from forming during the rising process. Cover with a clean towel and place in the preheated oven, (which has been turned off). The oven should not be hot, just slightly warmer than room temperature. Allow dough to rise for 1 1/2 hours.

5. Butter four loaf pans. Remove the dough from the oven and turn it onto a buttered kneading board. Using a sharp knife, cut the dough into 12 portions. Using 3 portions at a time, roll each piece by hand on the board to form finger shapes about 9 in. or 23 cm. in length and about 2 in. or 5 cm. in diameter. Place the three fingers side by side on the board about 1 in. or 2 cm. apart and pinch them together at one end. Loosely braid the 3 strands of dough and tuck the dough under at the opposite end. Place the braided dough in the buttered loaf pans. Continue this process with the other pieces of dough. You will have four loaves. The braiding should be evenly done. Brush the top of each with melted butter or pat the top of each with buttered fingers. Cover loaves with a clean towel and allow to rise at room temperature for one hour before baking. After the dough has risen, brush the surface of each loaf with beaten egg yolks and sprinkle with sesame seeds. Bake in a 300 degree F or 150° C preheated oven for one hour. The loaves will double in size and become a rich golden brown color. The sesame seeds will become toasted. Remove from the oven and cool before removing from the pans. You will be amazed at the look and the taste!

Note: The above is the traditional recipe and method for Greek Easter Bread, however, you may add dark raisins to the kneading process and the end result will be a rich and delicious raisin bread.

DAIRY PRODUCTS
AND
MAYONNAISE

ABOUT FETA CHEESE

Feta cheese is sold at almost all supermarkets. It is always found in Mediterranean and Greek grocery stores. There are a variety of different feta cheeses on the market. Each type should be sampled before purchasing, as they differ considerably in flavor. Ask for a sample of each type and choose the one you prefer.

Feta cheese must be stored correctly to ensure freshness and taste. The correct way to store it is to place it in a covered container in your refrigerator, submerged in a liquid called "brine". Brine is easily made from water and salt. Place cold water in a saucepan and add salt. The amount of salt added to the water is completely a preference in taste. If the water is saltier, the feta cheese will be saltier. If the water is milder, the flavor of the cheese will be milder. Bring the water and salt to a rapid boil for 2 minutes and remove from heat and cool to room temperature before adding to the cheese. The reason for boiling the water and salt is to ensure that all bacteria are eliminated from the water. If the salt water is used without boiling, the surface of the cheese will become soft and mushy during storage. Wash the feta after it comes from the store. Place the cheese in a clean container, such as a plastic container which has an air-tight top and cover it with the cooled salt water. Place in the refrigerator. The cheese will remain fresh and tasty and will keep its texture for as long as two weeks.

HOME-MADE,
UNRIPENED MILD CHEESE

| 12 cups | homogenized milk (2% may be used) | 3 litres |
| 6 | rennet tablets (sold at health food stores) | |

BRINE

| 2 cups | water | 500 mL |
| | salt to taste | |

METHOD:

1. Place the milk in a large, deep saucepan (preferably heavy stainless steel), and simmer over medium heat until the milk reaches boiling temperature. Stir occasionally to prevent the bottom from sticking. When the milk comes to a full boil, it will immediately begin to rise. Quickly remove the milk from the heat and allow to cool at room temperature. The milk must be watched at all times; failure to do this will result in the milk spilling over.

2. Place the rennet tables in a small bowl and crush to a powder, using a spoon. Add about 1 cup or 250 mL of the cooled milk. Stir the milk and tablets until they are completely dissolved. Gradually add this mixture into the rest of the cooled milk. Stir well. Place the milk back over moderately high heat and stir occasionally in one direction. As the temperature of the milk rises, cheese curds will form and will separate from the liquid (whey). When the milk reaches a boiling point, remove from the heat. The curds will be completely separated from the whey.

3. Take a large, clean cheesecloth and fold it in half, creating even smaller holes in the cloth. Place the cheesecloth over a large bowl; be sure that there is excess cloth over the edges of the bowl. Gently pour the curds and whey into the cheesecloth. Carefully lift the cloth, bringing the corners together to form a bag. Discard the whey; the curds will remain. Squeeze as much of the liquid from the whey as possible. Pull and tighten the cloth together at the top, causing the curds to be compressed. Place a clean flat dish or bowl over the cloth containing the curds and add weight The weight will force all of the excess liquid from the cheese and cause the curds to come together to form a cheese ball. Place in the refrigerator for at least eight hours, under pressure. Remove from the refrigerator and take the cheese from the cloth. It will be a firm round shape. At this point, the cheese is completely unsalted (sweet). The cheese is stored in brine to keep it moist and fresh.

4. Place 2 cups of cold water in a saucepan. Add salt to taste. The extent of saltiness of the brine will be the same as the saltiness of the cheese, as the cheese is kept in the brine. Cool to room temperature. Slice the cheese in wedges or slices and place in a sealable plastic container. Cover with the cooled brine and place the lid, tightly on the container. Refrigerate. This is the traditional, homemade, unripened mild cheese. Enjoy!

HOME-MADE PLAIN YOGHURT (TRADITIONAL GREEK METHOD)

Plain yoghurt is a very important part of traditional Greek cooking. It also provides a large percentage of calcium in their diet. It is very often eaten on its own with bread, as a main dish and more often served as a condiment with many different Greek main dishes and pitas. For the reason that it is eaten in such great quantity, many Greek people still make their own home-made yoghurt. It is a simple method which must always start with a culture. Commercially sold, unflavored yoghurt, purchased at a supermarket may be used as culture. After the initial culture, obtained this way, each time yoghurt is made at home, about $1/2$ cup or 125 mL is always reserved to be used as culture for the next batch. Homogenized milk produces a richer flavored yoghurt but 2% milk may also be used.

6 cups	fresh milk	1 $1/2$ litres
$1/2$ cup	culture	

METHOD:

1. Place cold milk in a large pot. Bring the milk to a boil over low heat to ensure it does not burn on the bottom. Stir the milk regularly. Do not leave the milk unattended as it will boil over and spill. Once the milk comes to a boil, it will rise very quickly. The moment it begins to rise in the pot, remove it at once from the heat and set it aside to cool.

2. The milk should be slightly warmer than room temperature, about 105° F or 40° C when mixing it to the culture. Place the culture in a small bowl and stir until very smooth. Gradually add about 1 cup or 250 mL of the cooled milk to the culture, stirring constantly. When the culture and the milk are completely combined, slowly add to the rest of the cooled milk and stir well until completely blended. Pour the milk mixture into a deep vessel with a cover. Use glass, pottery or plastic. Do not use aluminum. Cover and do not mix again. Gently wrap the covered vessel in a tablecloth and place on a smooth surface at room temperature. Do not move or unwrap for 8 - 10 hours. After the time has passed, remove the tablecloth and remove the cover. The yoghurt will be set but not very firm. It will still be soft but should be completely set. Place the cover back on the vessel and refrigerate until cold.

HOME-MADE TZATZIKI

Tzatziki is made from yoghurt. It is a simple process. Place a double layer of cheesecloth in a large bowl, lining the bowl completely and allowing the edges of the cheesecloth to hang over the sides of the bowl. Pour 1 1/2 litres of home-made yoghurt into the cheesecloth. Bring the sides of the cheesecloth together to form a bag. Tie the cheesecloth together, just above the top of the yoghurt. Apply pressure to the top of the bag by placing a plate on top and sitting a heavy can on the plate for 12 - 18 hours. Moisture will be removed from the yoghurt, using this method and should be discarded regularly. The tzatziki should be kept in the refrigerator during this process. After 12 hours, open the bag and transfer the tzatziki into a bowl. The consistency will be similar to that of sour cream or a bit thicker. Stir the tzatziki until smooth. Tzatziki may be used as a spread for bread or mixed with crushed garlic and extra virgin olive oil to be served as traditional tzatziki dip. Tzatziki dip is commonly used to accompany many Greek dishes.

CREAMY HOME-MADE MAYONNAISE

1	whole fresh egg	
1/2 cup	oil, use only light olive oil or canola oil	125 mL
1 1/2 tsp	fresh squeezed lemon juice (not bottled)	8 mL

METHOD:

In an electric blender, place one whole fresh egg and beat at high speed. Very gradually add oil. Mixture will become light and creamy. Add the fresh lemon juice. Blend for an additional 10 seconds.

Variations:
This recipe may be used as traditional mayonnaise or may be flavored with a number of ingredients and served as accompaniments to meat and fish or vegetables.

DILL FLAVORED MAYONNAISE (Ideal for seafood)

Add 1/4 cup or 60 mL of finely chopped fresh dill weed to the finished mayonnaise.

ROASTED SWEET RED PEPPER MAYONNAISE
(Delicious as a dip with vegetables or crackers)

Add $1/4$ cup or 60 mL of finely chopped roasted red sweet bell peppers to the finished mayonnaise.

ROASTED GARLIC FLAVORED MAYONNAISE
(Delicious with barbecued fish or chicken)

Add 3 tbsp of soft roasted garlic and $1/2$ tsp salt (optional) to finished mayonnaise. This may be added to hot mashed potatoes for delicious roasted garlic mashed potatoes.

SMOKED SALMON FLAVORED MAYONNAISE
(A savoury mayonnaise, ideal when used as a dip)

Add $1/2$ cup chopped, boneless smoked salmon to the finished mayonnaise and continue to purée for about 15 seconds.

VEGETARIAN DISHES

LEMONY - TRADITIONAL STEWED GREEK POTATOES

8	large white potatoes, cut in half	
	or 16 small potatoes, washed and peeled	
4 tbsp	extra virgin olive oil	60 mL
3/4 cup	puréed, stewed tomatoes	180 mL
2 1/4 cups	water or chicken stock	560 mL
2 cloves	garlic, crushed	
1 1/2 tsp	dry oregano flakes	8 mL
1 tsp	Hungarian paprika	5 mL
1 tsp	fresh ground black pepper	5 mL
1 tsp	salt (optional)	5 mL
2 tbsp	grated or finely chopped white onion	30 mL
2 tbsp	fresh lemon juice (not bottled)	30 mL

METHOD:

1. Wash and peel potatoes. If large potatoes are used, cut them in half. Potatoes may also be cut into large wedge shapes.

2. In a large saucepan, combine stewed tomatoes, cold water or chicken stock, crushed garlic and all of the other spices. Add olive oil, chopped onion and fresh lemon juice. Add the raw potatoes.

3. Simmer over medium heat, covered until the potatoes are very soft. Most of the liquid will have evaporated and the sauce will thicken. Serve hot with any meat, fish or chicken dish. These delicious potatoes may be eaten on their own with fresh bread and a salad as a main dish.

VEGETARIAN MOUSSAKA WITH POTATOES, EGGPLANT AND ZUCCHINI

2	large, unpeeled eggplants, washed and cut in $^1/4$ in. or 1 cm. slices	
2	large, 8 in. or 20 cm. unpeeled zucchini, washed and cut in $^1/4$ in. slices	
4 tbsp	extra virgin olive oil	60 mL
1 cup	finely chopped white onion	250 mL
2 cloves	crushed garlic	
1 cup	tomato sauce	250 mL
$^1/3$ cup	finely chopped parsley	80 mL
6	large, white potatoes, peeled and sliced in $^1/4$ inch or 1 cm. slices	
2	eggs, well beaten	
$^1/2$ cup	bread crumbs	125 mL
$^1/2$ cup	fresh grated parmesan cheese	125 mL
1 tsp	fresh ground black pepper	5 mL
1 tsp	salt (optional)	5 mL
1 tsp	fresh ground cinnamon	5 mL
1 tsp	fresh ground allspice	5 mL
1 tsp	fresh ground nutmeg	5 mL
	Béchamel sauce for topping	

METHOD:

1. Brush the eggplant and zucchini slices with olive oil and brown in a non-stick pan. Just brown, do not overcook, they should remain somewhat firm. Set aside.

2. Sauté onion and garlic in a hot skillet with olive oil until soft. Add chopped parsley, tomato sauce and spices. Cook over medium heat for about 3 minutes. Remove from heat and cool. When mixture is completely cool, add beaten eggs and half of the bread crumbs. In a greased, rectangular baking dish, spread the remainder of the bread crumbs evenly over the bottom. Alternate layers of eggplant, zucchini and potato slices. Top with grated cheese. Pour béchamel sauce over the top and bake at 350° F or 175° C for about 45 minutes until golden brown and fluffy. This recipe may be served hot or cold. Don't forget the olives, feta cheese and crusty Greek bread. Yummy!

BÉCHAMEL SAUCE

5 tbsp	butter	75 mL
5 tbsp	flour	75 mL
1/4 cup	parmesan cheese	60 mL
4	egg yolks	
1 tsp	nutmeg	5 mL
4 cups	milk	1 litre

METHOD:

Combine butter and flour in a non-stick pan. Stirring constantly with a wire whip, add milk gradually. Cook and stir constantly until mixture thickens. Beat the egg yolks and add a small amount of the sauce, stirring continuously. Add egg mixture to the rest of the sauce, slowly. Carefully, add the grated cheese.

BAKED VEGETABLE CASSEROLE WITH PINE NUTTY RICE

1	small eggplant, unpeeled	
2	small zucchini, unpeeled	
1/2 cup	chopped white onion	125 mL
2 cloves	crushed garlic	
1/4 cup	fresh chopped parsley	60 mL
4 tbsp	extra virgin olive oil	60 mL
2 tsp	Hungarian paprika	10 mL
1 tbsp	dry oregano flakes	15 mL
2 tsp	fresh ground black pepper	10 mL
1 tsp	salt (optional)	5 mL
3	large, white potatoes, peeled and cut into wedges	
2 cups	partially cooked, fresh green beans	500 mL
2 cups	stewed tomatoes (these may be puréed if desired)	500 mL
3 cups	cooked white rice with toasted pine seeds	750 mL

METHOD:

1. In a large non-stick skillet containing olive oil, combine paprika, crushed garlic and all other spices. Add chopped onions. Sauté over medium heat until the onions begin to brown. Add the potato wedges and continue to cook over a moderately high heat until the potatoes begin to brown. Add the tomatoes and chopped parsley.

2. Partially cook fresh green beans and drain. Chop the eggplant and zucchini into medium size pieces and place them in a large casserole dish. Add the green beans. Pour the tomato, potato and onion mixture over the vegetables in the casserole dish and toss together until blended. Bake in an uncovered casserole dish at 400° F or 200° C for approximately 45 minutes to one hour or until vegetables are soft and golden brown.

3. Pan toast 1/4 cup or 60 mL of pine nuts in 2 tbsp or 30 mL of butter. Sauté until the pine nuts become a deep golden brown. Add nuts and melted butter to cooked white rice. (Brown rice may be substituted). Serve hot with the baked vegetable casserole.

FLUFFY MASHED POTATOES WITH CARAMELIZED LEEKS

6	large potatoes, cooked and mashed. If using new potatoes or red potatoes, skin may be left on.	
1 1/2 cups	fresh leeks, chopped finely (white part only)	375 mL
3 tbsp	butter or extra virgin olive oil	45 mL
1/4 cup	fresh, plain yoghurt	60 mL
1/2 tsp	fresh ground black pepper	3 mL
1 tsp	salt (optional)	5 mL
	Hungarian paprika or cayenne powder as a garnish	

METHOD:

1. Sauté leeks in butter or olive oil until they begin to turn golden brown. Remove from heat and add to mashed potatoes. Add yoghurt, salt and pepper.

2. Whip until smooth and place in a well-buttered casserole dish. Sprinkle with paprika. Cayenne powder may be used instead of paprika as a garnish if a more spicy flavor is desired. Bake in a hot, 450 degree F or 225° C oven, lightly browning the top, for approximately 15 minutes. Remove from the oven and serve hot, on its own or as a delicious accompaniment to any meal.

SAUTÉED FRESH GREEN BEANS WITH CARAMELIZED ONIONS

1 ¹/₂ lb	fresh green beans (not frozen)	650 grams
	(any type of fresh green beans will work)	
2 cups	finely chopped, white onion	500 mL
4 tbsp	extra virgin olive oil	60 mL
2 tsp	fresh ground black pepper	10 mL
2 tsp	salt (optional)	10 mL
1 cup	stewed tomatoes, chopped finely (optional)	250 mL

METHOD:

1. In a large saucepan containing olive oil, sauté chopped onions until they become caramelized or a deep golden brown color. Wash and chop the fresh green beans and add them to the cooked onions.

2. Sauté the green beans and onions over moderately high heat, stirring often and scraping the bottom of the pan to remove the coating on the bottom. Stir the coating through the beans during the cooking process. This adds additional caramelizing and exceptional flavor to the dish. Occasionally the bottom of the pan may seem to be very brown. At these points, add about 2 - 3 tbsp or 30 mL of cold water at a time to loosen onions which are sticking to the bottom. This occurrence is necessary in order to obtain the correct flavor. Continue to cook the beans until they are tender. Add salt and pepper to taste and just before the beans are cooked, add the tomatoes, (optional). If you are adding the tomatoes, sauté the beans and the tomatoes together for about ten minutes, stirring regularly.

3. This is an exceptionally flavorful dish which may be eaten on its own with roasted or stewed Greek potatoes and salad. It is also a delicious accompaniment when served as a vegetable.

DELICIOUS LEEK
AND POTATO PANCAKES

3 cups	finely shredded, starchy, white potatoes	750 mL
1 tbsp	white flour	
1/2 cup	finely chopped leeks (white part only)	125 mL
1 tbsp	extra virgin olive oil	15 mL
2	eggs, well beaten	
1 tsp	fresh ground black pepper	5 mL
1 tsp	salt (optional)	5 mL
	butter and olive oil for frying	

METHOD:

1. Finely shred raw potatoes and place in a large bowl. Add 2 beaten eggs, flour, salt and pepper to taste. In a skillet containing 1 tbsp olive oil, sauté chopped leeks until soft. Remove from heat and cool. Add cooled leeks to the shredded potato mixture. Combine all ingredients thoroughly.

2. Drop the potato and leek mixture by the tablespoonful into a hot, non-stick pan containing 1 tbsp or 15 mL each of olive oil and butter. Flatten slightly with the back of the spoon. Sauté over medium heat until the edges of the pancake begin to turn color around the edges. Using a spatula, carefully turn the pancakes over and cook until the potatoes are tender and golden brown.

3. Serve hot with home-made yoghurt or tzatziki. These pancakes may be made bite-size and served as a delicious canapé.

MACARONI ROTINI SALAD WITH
MARINATED CHICKEN BREAST, P. 37

FRIED EGGPLANT WITH GARLIC AND LEMON,
P. 98

MARINATED SALMON FILLETS WITH GARLIC AND FRESH DILL, p. 108

LENTILS WITH CARAMELIZED ONIONS AND WHITE RICE

1 cup	raw, uncooked brown lentils	250 mL
1 cup	uncooked, white rice	250 mL
^{1}/3 cup	extra virgin olive oil	160 mL
3 cups	white onions, slivered	750 mL
6 cups	water	1 ^{1}/2 litres
1 ^{1}/2 tsp	fresh ground black pepper	8 mL
1 tsp	salt (optional)	10 mL

METHOD:

1. Wash raw lentils thoroughly. Rinse and drain the water. In a large pot containing olive oil, sauté the onions until they are a very deep, golden brown color. The onions should be a very dark golden color, but not burned. This well-done cooking process of the onions adds the flavor to this dish. If desired, about ^{1}/4 cup or 60 mL of the cooked onions may be reserved to use as a garnish.

2. Add the washed, raw lentils to the onions and stir. Add water, salt and pepper. Cover and cook over medium heat for about 45 minutes until the lentils are cooked. Wash and drain rice and add to the cooked lentils. Simmer over moderate heat until the liquid is absorbed and the rice is light and fluffy, stirring often. When the water is evaporated and the rice is cooked, place in a serving platter and garnish with reserved onions.

3. This dish may be served warm or cold. It makes a delicious main dish when accompanied by a salad such as cucumber and tomato and fresh pita bread.

BAKED EGGPLANT AND FETA CHEESE CASSEROLE

2	medium size eggplants, unpeeled	
1/4 cup	milk	60 mL
2	eggs, well beaten	
	bread crumbs for dredging	
1 tsp	salt (optional)	5 mL
1 tsp	fresh ground black pepper	5 mL
4	cloves, crushed garlic	
4 tbsp	extra virgin olive oil	60 mL
2 tsp	dry oregano flakes	10 mL
3/4 cup	crumbled feta cheese	125 mL

METHOD:

1. Wash eggplant thoroughly and cut in 1/4 in. or 1 cm. slices. Combine the milk and egg in a small bowl and beat well. Dip slices of eggplant in the milk and egg mixture and dredge in bread crumbs, on both sides. Brown breaded eggplant slices in a non-stick pan brushed with olive oil. Over moderate heat, brown the eggplant evenly on both sides.

2. Remove the eggplant from the pan and place in an open casserole dish. Combine 2 tbsp olive oil, oregano flakes, crushed garlic and salt and pepper and brush the top of the eggplant. Sprinkle crumbled feta cheese over the top of the casserole and bake at 350° F or 175° C for about a half hour or until the cheese is turning golden brown.

3. This is a delicious vegetarian meal. Serve with fresh Greek bread and a fresh salad. Don't forget the olives!

BAKED RED KIDNEY BEAN CASSEROLE WITH NUTTY RICE

2 cups	red kidney beans (canned beans in liquid are ideal)	500 mL
1/4 cup	chopped celery hearts	60 mL
1/4 cup	chopped sweet, red bell peppers	60 mL
1/4 cup	chopped sweet, green bell peppers	60 mL
1/2 cup	chopped white onions	125 mL
3 tbsp	extra virgin olive oil	45 mL
2 cloves	crushed garlic	
2 cups	stewed tomatoes, chopped	500 mL
1 tbsp	dry oregano flakes	15 mL
2 tsp	Hungarian paprika	10 mL
2 tsp	fresh ground black pepper	10 mL
1 tsp	salt (optional)	5 mL
1 1/4 cup	toasted pine nuts (pan toasted in 2 tbsp or 30 mL butter)	60 mL
3 cups	cooked white rice (brown rice may be substituted)	750 mL

METHOD:

1. In a saucepan, combine olive oil, spices, crushed garlic and chopped vegetables. Sauté over medium heat until the onions are transparent. Add the kidney beans and the tomatoes.

2. Place the kidney beans together with all of the ingredients in a casserole dish. Bake for 35 to 40 minutes at 350° F or 175° C or until the casserole is bubbling and beginning to brown on the top.

3. In a non-stick pan, sauté pine nuts in butter, slowly, until golden brown. Remove and stir into 3 cups of cooked, drained rice. Serve hot with casserole.

4. Add a salad and fresh bread and this meal will become a favorite.

BARBECUED FRESH SARDINES WRAPPED IN GRAPE VINE LEAVES WITH OLIVE OIL AND FRESH LEMON

Fresh Sardines, cleaned and scaled. Heads and tales, preferably removed.

Preserved grape vine leaves. These may be purchased in any specialty Greek or Middle Eastern Grocery Store. I find the ones imported from California are very good.

METHOD:

1. Thoroughly wash and dry the cleaned and scaled fish.

2. Using two or three large grape vine leaves which come bottled in brine, place them on a flat surface with the stem at the bottom. Remove the stem portion which is tough and unnecessary with a sharp knife. Place about three large leaves beside each other, overlapping slightly. They may be washed from the brine to remove salty flavour, if preferred. This is not, however, essential. If you prefer a saltier taste, use straight from the jar. Place the fish at the bottom of the leaves and roli the leaves around the fish from the bottom to the top. Most of the fish will be covered by the leaves.

3. Place on a preheated, very hot barbecue grill which has been lightly oiled to prevent sticking. Using tongs, turn the vine leaf wrapped sardines often to ensure even cooking. Fish will be done when vine leaves are slightly charred. Cooking time will be about eight to ten minutes. When fish is cooked, drizzle extra virgin olive oil and fresh squeezed lemon over the entire surface of the wrapped sardines. Remove from grill and serve immediately.

4. This dish is delicious with Greek Village Salad and fresh bread.

SAVORY GREEK PIZZA WITH BROWNED EGGPLANT, RED AND YELLOW PEPPERS AND BLACK OLIVES

Home-made pita dough recipe

$^1/_3$ cup	tomato purée	60 mL
$^1/_3$ cup	finely chopped stewed tomatoes	60 mL
$^1/_3$ cup	water	60 mL
3 tbsp	extra virgin olive oil	45 mL
3 tsp	dry oregano flakes	15 mL
1 tsp	salt (optional)	5 mL
1 tsp	fresh ground black pepper	5 mL
$^1/_2$ cup	pitted calamata olives (not canned)	125 mL
$^1/_2$ cup	sweet red bell peppers,	125 mL
$^1/_2$ cup	sweet yellow bell peppers,	125 mL
1 $^1/_2$ cup	eggplant strips	375 mL
1 $^1/_2$ cup	feta cheese, crumbled	375 mL

METHOD:

1. Wash and dry the peppers, remove the stems and the seeds. Cut into thin strips. Wash eggplant and remove the stem. Do not peel. Cut eggplant in slices and then into thin strips. Place the peppers and the eggplant in a non-stick pan containing 1 tbsp extra virgin olive oil. Sauté over moderately high heat until the vegetables are beginning to brown. Remove from heat and cool.

2. Combine tomato purée, stewed tomatoes and water in a small bowl. Add 1 tbsp olive oil, 2 tsp oregano and salt and pepper. Stir well.

3. Prepare the home-made pita dough recipe and press out by hand or roll out, using a rolling pin to fit a 16 in. or 40 cm. round pizza pan. Spread the tomato mixture evenly over the crust. Arrange the browned eggplant and pepper strips on the pizza and sprinkle with crumbled feta cheese. Drizzle with 1 tbsp olive oil and 1 tsp oregano flakes. Allow to proof in pan for 20 minutes before baking. Bake in a hot oven at 375° F or 190° C for approximately twenty-five minutes or until golden brown.

4. Remove from the oven and slice into wedges. Hot or cold, with a green salad, a tasty vegetarian dinner. This pizza may also be cut into bite-size pieces and served as delicious canapés.

FRIED EGGPLANT WITH GARLIC AND LEMON

1	large eggplant, unpeeled, cut into $1/4$ in. or 1 cm. slices extra virgin olive oil for frying eggplant.	
3 - 4 cloves crushed garlic		
2 tbsp	fresh squeezed lemon juice (not bottled)	30 mL
1 tbsp	extra virgin olive oil	15 mL
1 tsp	salt (optional)	5 mL
$1/2$ cup	finely chopped, fresh parsley	125 mL

METHOD:

1. Thoroughly wash the eggplant and cut off the stem portion. Do not peel. Slice in $1/4$ inch slices and brush on both sides with extra virgin olive oil. Brown the eggplant in a non-stick pan until golden brown on both sides.

2. Arrange cooked eggplant on a decorative serving dish. Combine the lemon juice, 1 tbsp extra virgin olive oil, salt and crushed garlic. Drizzle over the eggplant and sprinkle with fresh chopped parsley.

SPINACH AND RICOTTA CHEESE LASAGNE

1 pkg	lasagne noodles, parboiled	375 mL
2 1/2 cups	ricotta cheese	
1/2 cup	fresh grates Romano cheese	125 mL
	(parmesan may be used)	
3 cups	coarsely grated mozzarella cheese	750 mL
4	whole eggs, beaten	
1 lb	fresh spinach (not frozen)	450 grams
1 cup	canned tomato paste	450 mL
3 1/2 cups	cold water	675 mL
3 cloves	crushed garlic	
2 tsp	dry oregano flakes	10 mL
1 tsp	dry basil	5 mL
4 tbsp	extra virgin olive oil	60 mL

METHOD:

1. Parboil the lasagne noodles until they begin to soften. Remove noodles and run under cold water to prevent them from sticking together . Thoroughly wash and chop fresh spinach. Steam until soft and drain. Be sure all water is completely removed, if necessary squeeze it dry by hand.

2. In a large bowl containing ricotta cheese, and grated Romano or parmesan cheese, add beaten eggs and cooked, drained spinach. Combine all ingredients well.

3. Combine tomato paste, water, crushed garlic, olive oil and spices. Bring to a boil and remove from heat. Cool to room temperature. Spread about one cup of the tomato sauce on the bottom of an ungreased, stainless steel, glass, or ceramic lasagne pan. Alternate layers of lasagne noodles, cheese/spinach mixture and grated mozzarella cheese.

4. After noodles and filling are used, gently pour the remainder of the sauce over the lasagne, allowing it to run down into the lasagne. Top with mozzarella cheese and cover tightly with aluminum foil. Bake slowly in a moderate oven temperature of 350° F or 175° C for approximately 1 1/2 hours. Check the lasagne after about

1 hour. Cover and continue to cook for an additional $^1/_2$ hour or until it is cooked. When lasagne is ready it will have risen and become fluffy. Test to ensure that the center of the lasagne is cooked. Remove from the oven, remove the foil and allow it to sit at room temperature for about five minutes before serving. Serve hot with fresh bread and a salad. A tasty and satisfying vegetarian dish.

MOUTH-WATERING FALAFEL ON PITA BREAD WITH FRESH VEGGIES AND TAHINI SAUCE

Falafel recipes vary. I have found that the most delicious falafel is also the most convenient. It can be purchased in any Mediterranean specialty store by its name, Falafel. It comes pre-packaged as a ready-to-use mix. Only water needs to be added and this package of powdered, dried legumes, mixed with a wonderful blend of aromatic herbs and spices quickly transforms itself into a fluffy combination of delicious and nutritious ingredients, ready for preparation. There are, of course, several brands on the market. Some are better than others. Try them and choose your favorite.

No matter what brand you prefer, the preparation is the same. You just add enough cool (not cold) water to completely moisten the falafel. It should have a slightly runny consistency and should not initially be dry enough to form a ball or burger shape. Combine the mix with water and stir well. Allow it to sit at room temperature for about 15 to 20 minutes. The mixture will absorb the water and will become fluffy. After the mixture has risen, it will be the correct consistency to shape.

METHOD:

1. Take a small amount of the mixture in your hand and firmly press it together to form a small burger or ball about the size of a walnut.

2. Deep-fry falafel balls in hot canola oil (360° F or 175° C), turning constantly to prevent overcooking. When they are crisp and golden brown in color, remove and drain, to remove excess oil. Allow to cool on paper towels.

3. Place two or three falafel in a pita bread; they may be broken, if desired. Top with a fresh and incredibly flavorful sauce, (recipe follows). Roll up the pita bread and sauce and you are in for an amazing taste experience!

CRUNCHY, FRESH VEGETABLE AND TAHINI SAUCE FOR FALAFEL

1/2	small head of iceberg lettuce, chopped	
2 cups	firm, red tomatoes,	500 mL
1 cup	garlic, dill pickles, chopped	250 mL
1 cup	chopped, fresh parsley leaves	250 mL
4 cloves	crushed garlic	
1/2 cup	sesame seed purée (tahini)	125 mL
1/3 cup	cold water	80 mL
1/4 cup	fresh lemon juice (not bottled)	60 mL
1 tsp	salt (optional)	5 mL
1 tsp	fresh ground black pepper	5 mL

METHOD:

1. Combine lettuce, chopped tomatoes, chopped pickles and chopped parsley in a large bowl.

2. In an electric blender, combine tahini, fresh lemon juice, crushed garlic, salt and pepper and cold water. Blend at high speed until the mixture becomes smooth. It should have the consistency of a milkshake. If too thick, add more water and lemon juice. If too thin, add a bit more tahini.

3. Add the tahini sauce to the chopped vegetables and toss using two spoons thoroughly until all the vegetables are evenly coated. The sauce will be chunky and should have a tangy, lemony flavor.

4. Use this sauce to top a falafel sandwich or serve as an accompaniment to falafel when served on a dish. Falafel is traditionally eaten with fresh pita bread. This dish is amazingly fresh and flavorful.

MAIN COURSES

LAMB

Lamb is traditionally the meat most often eaten in Greece. A variety of types and cuts of lamb are readily available to us. Lamb may be bought frozen or fresh at any butcher shop or supermarket. It should be known that lamb varies in flavor and for this reason, it is important to sample the different varieties, in order that you may decide the type of lamb and the flavor you prefer. Frozen, imported lamb has a much stronger aroma and flavor, however this may be your preference. Fresh, unfrozen, local lamb has a much lighter, and more delicate taste and a far more subtle aroma. Authentic Greek dishes are always prepared with fresh, local lamb. Traditionally, frozen lamb is not used, simply because there was always fresh lamb available in Greece. Therefore, to achieve the true flavor of the lamb dishes in this book, it is my opinion that the use of fresh, local lamb, will enable you to achieve the authentic taste. Lamb is a very fatty meat. When cooking with lamb, ensure that as much of the excess fat as possible is cut off before cooking. When roasting a leg or shoulder of lamb, for example, most of the fat should be removed and fresh lemon juice should be squeezed over the roast, prior to cooking. The lemon cuts any greasy taste which could occur and promotes a lighter flavor. Although in some countries lamb is served rare, in Greece, lamb is traditionally served well-done. This well-done method creates a crisp outer layer on the roast lamb which, in combination with the herbs and spices accomplishes the authentic flavor of the renowned, Greek roast lamb.

BEEF

When choosing beef for casserole recipes, it is best to select stewing beef which includes a bone; for example short ribs, blade roast or beef shank. Ask your butcher for the cuts of stewing beef which include a bone. As well as adding flavor and vitamins to the dish, the meat next to the bone is always more tender and juicy. Be sure that the meat does not include excessive fat, however a small amount of fat keeps the meat tender. Boneless, totally fatless stewing beef tends to be more dry and less tender.

PORK

When choosing pork for your recipes, use lean pork. Softer, less dry pork comes from the butt or leg area and slightly drier meat comes from the loin. Pork is a very flavorful meat and is used in a variety of recipes in Greek cuisine.

CHICKEN

When chicken is used in the chicken casserole recipes in this book, the best results will come from using a whole chicken which you cut into pieces yourself. Boiling the entire chicken adds incredible flavor as well as vitamins to the dish. The meat should be separated and the bones and the skin should always be discarded when the chicken is cooked. Choosing boneless chicken pieces for a casserole will contribute very little flavor, and some cuts, such as boiled boneless chicken breast may be tough. Chicken skin may be removed prior to boiling, as chicken skin does not add flavor, only fat.

FISH

Traditionally, deep, cold water fish has been a very large and important part of the Greek diet. Omega-3 fatty acids are found in fish oils. Medical studies have shown that including fish in the daily diet can be extremely beneficial to good health. The Greeks prepare fish in a variety of ways which include broiling, barbecuing or frying on its own, or in stews and casseroles containing fresh herbs and vegetables. This wide diversity in the preparation of fish makes it easy and enjoyable to eat fish often.

BASIC GREEK MARINADE

The basic Greek marinade is the marinade that creates the authentic flavor. It is used for lamb, beef, pork, chicken and fish. The quantities will vary according to the amount of meat being marinated. You can add or subtract from the quantities of ingredients used. If you use all of the ingredients, however, the flavor result will always be correct.

olive oil
crushed garlic
oregano, dry flakes or fresh
pinch of dry mint
fresh ground black pepper
salt
fresh squeezed lemon juice (never bottled)

Enjoy!

Tender Beef and Caramelized Onion Casserole

2 1/2 lb	stewing beef	1 1/4 kg
3 tbsp	butter or extra virgin live oil	45 mL
3 cloves	crushed garlic	
3 tsp	Hungarian paprika	15 mL
3	whole bay leaves	
1 1/2 tsp	fresh ground allspice powder	8 mL
1 tsp	fresh ground cinnamon powder	5 mL
1 cup	dry red wine	250 mL
2 tsp	salt (optional)	10 mL
2 tsp	fresh ground black pepper	10 mL
2 lb	whole white baby onions or slivered white onions	1 litre
1 1/2 cups	fresh carrots, coarsely chopped	375 mL
1 1/2 cups	stewed tomatoes, chopped	375 mL
4 cups	beef stock	1 litre

Method:

1. In a large skillet containing melted butter or olive oil, add onions and crushed garlic. Sauté over medium heat until the onions begin to turn a deep golden brown color and caramelize. Add the paprika and other spices. Add the tomatoes, wine and the bay leaves. Add the chopped carrots.

2. Bring stewing beef to a boil in 4 cups of beef stock. Cover and simmer over medium heat for about 2 - 2 1/2 hours or until the meat is very soft and tender. The liquid will have reduced considerably. Add enough additional beef stock to make up 2 cups or 500 mL Remove the beef from the stock and place it in a deep casserole dish. A glass dish works very well, as it ensures even cooking. Strain the 2 cups of beef stock through a sieve into the onion and tomato mixture.

3. Add the onion mixture to the casserole dish and combine with the meat. Place in a hot 375 degree F or 190 degree C oven, uncovered, for approximately 1 1/2 hours or until the top of the casserole is browned and most of the liquid is absorbed. Cheek the casserole frequently, less cooking time may be necessary. Remove the bay leaves. Serve with fluffy mashed potatoes and a leafy salad. Savory and delicious!

BROILED FILLET OF SOLE WITH SAVORY SALMON STUFFING

6	boneless, skinless sole fillets	
1 cup	boneless, skinless fresh salmon fillets, salmon should be very finely chopped or minced	250 mL
$1/2$ cup	dry bread crumbs	125 mL
$1/2$ cup	water or fish stock	60 mL
1 $1/2$ tbsp	baby green onions, finely chopped	25 mL
1 $1/2$ tbsp	chopped celery hearts, finely chopped	25 mL
1 tbsp	fresh chopped parsley leaves	15 mL
1 tbsp	fresh chopped dill weed	15 mL
1 tbsp	toasted, pine nuts	15 mL
3 tbsp	melted butter	45 mL
2 cloves	crushed garlic	
$1/2$ tsp	dry oregano flakes	3 mL
$1/2$ tsp	salt (optional)	3 mL
$1/2$ tsp	Hungarian paprika	3 mL
1	whole egg, well beaten melted butter for basting home-made, dill flavored mayonnaise as a condiment	

METHOD:

1. Combine green onions, crushed garlic, chopped celery and spices in a non-stick skillet containing 2 tbsp of melted butter. Sauté over medium heat for approximately 2 - 3 minutes. Add bread crumbs and fish stock. Add parsley and dill. Add toasted pine nuts (pan toasted in 1 tsp butter until golden brown). Combine all the ingredients and set aside to cool. When mixture is completely cool, add the minced, uncooked salmon fillets and the beaten egg. Blend thoroughly.

2. Wash and dry the sole fillets and place about 2 tbsp or 30 mL of the stuffing mixture at one end of each fillet. Carefully roll the fillet in a jelly roll fashion. Secure the end with toothpicks.

3. Place the stuffed sole fillets in a shallow, buttered baking dish and baste with melted butter. Sprinkle with paprika for color. Bake at 375° F or 190° C for approximately 12 - 15 minutes until the fish is flaky.

4. Remove from oven, remove toothpicks and serve immediately with plenty of fresh lemon wedges. Ideal when served with rice or potatoes and any veggie side dish. Don't forget the home-made, dill flavored mayonnaise!

MARINATED SALMON FILLETS WITH GARLIC AND FRESH DILL
FRESH SALMON STEAKS OR BONELESS FILLETS

Marinade

1/4 cup	extra virgin olive oil	60 mL
1/4 cup	fresh squeezed lemon juice (not bottled)	60 mL
2 cloves	crushed garlic	
2 tbsp	fresh dill weed, finely chopped	30 mL
1 tsp	fresh ground black pepper	5 mL
1 tsp	salt (optional)	5 mL
	home made dill flavored mayonnaise	
	fresh lemon wedges	

METHOD:

1. Combine olive oil, fresh lemon juice and crushed garlic in a small bowl. Add fresh chopped dill weed and stir all ingredients until well blended.

2. Place salmon steaks or fillets in a shallow, glass pan and cover with marinade. Tightly cover with plastic wrap and refrigerate for at least eight hours. Remove the fish from the marinade and barbecue or grill over moderately high heat turning once. Cooking time is approximately 4 - 5 minutes on each side. Fish is done when it comes apart easily in flakes when touched with a fork.

3. This fish may be served hot or cold as a main dish. Accompany it with a colorful salad and roast potatoes or rice. Be sure to include plenty of fresh lemon wedges and of course, home-made dill flavored mayonnaise.

CHICKEN SOUVLAKI, P. 149

PECAN BAKLAVA. P. 156

SEAFOOD CROQUETTES WITH SPICY HOT BANANA PEPPER SAUCE

1 cup	flaked, cooked cold water fish, any type	250 mL
1 cup	cooked shrimp, finely chopped or minced	250 mL
1 cup	cooked, shredded crab meat	250 mL
1/2 cup	fresh green onions, finely chopped	125 mL
1/4 cup	fresh parsley, finely chopped	60 mL
2 tbsp	fresh dill weed, finely chopped	30 mL
1 tsp	fresh ground black pepper	5 mL
1 tsp	salt (optional)	5 mL
1 tsp	garlic powder (not garlic salt)	5 mL
1 cup	dry, unseasoned bread crumbs	250 mL
2	whole eggs, well beaten, flour for dredging, canola oil for flying	

Sauce

2-3	hot banana peppers	
2 cups	fresh ripe tomatoes, or stewed tomatoes, chopped	500 mL
4 cloves	crushed garlic	
2 tbsp	extra virgin olive oil	30 mL
1 tsp	salt (optional)	5 mL

METHOD:

1. In a large bowl, combine fish, shrimp, crab meat, green onions, parsley and dill. Add all of the spices, the bread crumbs and the eggs. Mix thoroughly. Mixture should have a pasty consistency, thick enough to form croquettes. If the mixture is too wet, additional bread crumbs may be added. If too dry, add a few drops of water or fish stock.

2. Take a small amount of the mixture in your hand and form croquettes, fingers or ball shapes. Dredge in flour, evenly on all sides and fry or deep fry in hot canola oil until golden brown and crisp on the outside. Remove from oil and drain on paper towels.

3. Wash and dry peppers. Remove seeds and stem. Chop into small pieces and sauté, together with crushed garlic, over medium heat in a non-stick pan containing 2 tbsp extra virgin olive oil until they begin to turn golden brown. Add tomatoes and salt. Simmer together for about five minutes and remove from heat. Purée the pepper sauce in a food processor and serve with cooked seafood croquettes. Sweet peppers may be substituted for hot, if desired. Serve with potatoes or rice and a colorful salad. Don't forget the feta cheese. Delicious!

BROILED COD FILLETS WITH GARLIC BUTTER AND FRESH PARSLEY FRESH, BONELESS COD FILLETS

4 tbsp	melted butter	60 mL
2 cloves	crushed garlic	
2 tsp	Hungarian paprika	10 mL
1/4 cup	fresh squeezed lemon juice (not bottled)	60 mL
1 tsp	salt (optional)	5 mL
1 tsp	fresh ground black pepper	5 mL
1/2 cup	fresh parsley leaves, finely chopped	125 mL

METHOD:

1. Thoroughly wash the fish fillets and place them in a shallow baking dish.

2. Combine crushed garlic with melted butter and paprika, and drizzle over fish. Pour the fresh lemon juice over the fillets. Sprinkle the fresh chopped parsley, evenly. Add salt and pepper to taste.

3. Bake at 350° F or 175° C for approximately 12 - 15 minutes or until the fish is flaky to the touch.

4. This fish is delicious when served with rice or potatoes. For a tasty and different combination, try serving with sautéed fresh green beans and caramelized onions and hummus dip. Include plenty of fresh pita bread.

STUFFED BABY EGGPLANTS WITH GROUND LAMB, WHITE RICE AND PINE NUTS

6 - 8	baby eggplants	
1 lb	ground, fresh local lamb	450 grams
$1/2$ cup	white onion, finely chopped	375 mL
$1/4$ cup	toasted pine nuts	60 mL
$1/4$ cup	fresh chopped parsley leaves	60 mL
$1/4$ cup	sweet red bell pepper	60 mL
4 cloves	crushed garlic	
2 tbsp	extra virgin olive oil	30 mL
1 tsp	fresh ground black pepper	5 mL
1 tsp	salt (optional)	5 mL
1 tsp	fresh ground allspice powder	5 mL
1 tsp	cinnamon	5 mL
1 $1/2$ cups	white rice, parboiled	375 mL
2 $1/4$ cups	stewed tomatoes, puréed	560 mL
1 $1/4$ cups	beef, vegetable or chicken stock	185 mL

METHOD:

1. Thoroughly wash and dry the eggplants. Cut off the end together with the stem. Using a hollowing utensil or a sharp ended, long spoon, slowly hollow out the eggplant, leaving a $1/2$ in. or 1 $1/2$ cm. wall. Be careful to not puncture the wall of the eggplant. Retain the eggplant pulp which has been removed.

2. In a skillet containing olive oil, add the onions and peppers. Add 2 cloves of crushed garlic, spices. Sauté over medium heat until onions become transparent. Add chopped eggplant pulp and chopped parsley. Combine all ingredients and add the partially cooked rice. Add toasted pine seeds which have been pan toasted in 2 tbsp or 20 mL of butter until they are golden brown. Remove from heat and set aside to cool. When the rice mixture is totally cooled, add the uncooked, ground lamb. Combine all ingredients thoroughly, by hand.

3. Carefully, stuff the hollowed out eggplants with the rice and meat filling by hand or by using a long handled spoon, ensuring not to puncture the wall of the eggplant. Do not overstuff each eggplant. Keep in mind that the rice will need space to expand during the cooking process.

4. Place the eggplants in a casserole dish. Combine the tomato purée and the stock. Add 2 cloves of crushed garlic and salt and pepper to taste. Pour around the eggplants. Cover the casserole dish tightly, and bake at 375° F or 190° C for approximately 45 minutes or until the rice is fluffy and the eggplants are soft. About half of the liquid will be evaporated. Serve hot from the oven with fresh bread and cold plain yoghurt.

BAKED LAMB AND SUMMER VEGETABLE MEDLEY

2 lb	lean, local stewing lamb	1 kg
6 cups	cold water	1 1/2 litres
1 cup	coarsely chopped white onion	250 mL
1 medium	eggplant, unpeeled	
2 cups	zucchini, unpeeled	500 mL
2 cups	fresh green beans (not frozen)	500 mL
4 medium	white potatoes	
1/2 cup	chopped fresh parsley leaves	125 mL
2 cups	stewed tomatoes, chopped or puréed	500 mL
4 cloves	crushed garlic	
2 tbsp	extra virgin olive oil	30 mL
2 tsp	salt (optional)	10 mL
2 tsp	fresh ground black pepper	10 mL
4 tsp	Hungarian paprika	20 mL

METHOD:

1. Thoroughly wash the lamb meat and remove any excess fat. Place the meat in a large pot and cover with cold water. Bring to a boil and reduce heat. Simmer over medium heat for about two hours until the meat is very tender. Remove from heat and cool. Retain the liquid.

2. In a heavy, non-stick skillet containing olive oil, combine chopped onions and potatoes with crushed garlic, paprika, black pepper and salt. Sauté over moderately high heat, turning constantly until the onions and potatoes begin to brown. Add the remaining vegetables, except for the green beans, and continue to sauté for an additional five minutes until all the vegetables have begun to brown nicely. Add the chopped or puréed tomatoes. Place fresh green beans in a saucepan with cold water. Bring to a boil and cook for 2 minutes. Remove the beans and rinse under cold water to retain their color. Drain and set aside.

3. Place the cooked lamb in a large, rectangular casserole dish. Cover the meat with the green beans. Add vegetable mixture, tomato and 2 cups of liquid used to boil the lamb. Toss lightly in the casserole dish, ensure all ingredients are mixed together. Bake, uncovered in a hot oven 375° F or 190° C for approximately one hour or until the vegetables are golden brown and the potatoes are soft in the center. Serve immediately with fresh crusty Greek bread. Delicious when accompanied by fresh cold yoghurt.

TANGY STUFFED GRAPE LEAVES WITH FRESH GROUND LAMB AND WHITE RICE

1 1/2 lb	fresh ground local lamb (lean beef may be substituted)	675 grams
2 jars	prepared grape leaves, available in all Greek grocery stores	
1 cup	white onion, very finely chopped	250 mL
2 cloves	crushed garlic	
2 tbsp	olive oil	30 mL
1/2 cup	fresh parsley leaves, finely chopped	125 mL
4 tsp	dry oregano flakes	20 mL
2 tsp	fresh ground black pepper	10 mL
4 tbsp	extra virgin olive oil	60 mL
3 cups	partially cooked, short grain white rice	750 mL
1/2 cup	olive oil and	125 mL
1 1/2 cups	water, for boiling	375 mL
1/3 cup	fresh lemon juice (not bottled)	80 mL

METHOD:

1. Grape leaves are used directly from the jar. Remove them from the water in the jar and unfold them, using one at a time. With a sharp knife, cut off the stem portion of the leaf and discard it.

2. Place the rice in a saucepan and cover with cold water. Bring to a boil and simmer for about 2 - 3 minutes, or just until the rice begins to soften slightly. Strain the rice from the hot water and run under cold water. Set aside to cool. Place cooled, drained rice in a large bowl. Add raw ground lamb, chopped onion, crushed garlic, chopped parsley and spices. Add 2 tbsp olive oil. Blend all ingredients by hand. The mixture should stick together when pressed in one hand. If it is too dry, add a few drops of cold water and mix.

3. Place about 1 tbsp or 15 mL of the meat and rice mixture at the bottom of each grape leaf. Roll the leaf from the bottom up, tucking the edges inward, toward the center, continuing to roll, snugly to the top of the leaf you should have a

slightly rectangular shaped, firm roll. The jar of leaves will contain a few very small leaves. These leaves are too small to roll. Place them on the bottom of a deep, stainless steel saucepan, drizzled with 2 tbsp or 15 mL of olive oil. The leaves should completely cover the bottom of the saucepan. This will prevent any sticking during the cooking process. Arrange the grape leaf rolls in layers, snugly touching. Once the first layer is complete, repeat the second and the third layer in the same way until all of the rice and meat mixture and all of the grape leaves are used.

4. Combine approximately a $1/2$ cup olive oil with cold water and fresh lemon juice and mix thoroughly. Pour gently over the stuffed grape leaves, barely covering the leaves. Place three inverted plates, fitting almost to the edges of the saucepan over the leaves. This weight prevents the stuffed grape leaves from opening during cooking. Cover tightly and bring to a boil over moderate heat. Reduce heat to low and continue to cook for approximately 1 $1/2$ hours. Remove cover and check often for liquid content. If liquid has been absorbed, add more of the remaining liquid in small amounts. After about 1 $1/2$ hours, test to see if the rice is cooked. If the rice is completely fluffy and soft, remove from heat and allow the grape leaves to sit, covered for about 15 minutes. At this time, carefully tip the saucepan, draining all excess liquid. After the liquid has been removed, cover the saucepan again and allow it to sit for an additional 15 minutes. Remove the plates used as weights. Invert a wide, shallow bowl over the top of the saucepan. Very carefully turn the saucepan up side down allowing the stuffed grape leaves to fall into the dish. This method prevents breakage from occurring when trying to remove the grape leaves one at a time.

5. Drizzle with extra virgin olive oil and fresh lemon juice. Cool to room temperature and cover tightly before refrigerating. Serve cold as a main dish or as an appetizer. Your guests will be amazed!

Traditional Baked Lamb with Fresh Spinach Casserole

2 ¹/₂ lb	fresh stewing lamb	1 kg
2 tbsp	extra virgin olive oil	30 mL
6 cups	water	1 ¹/₂ litres
1 ¹/₂ lb	fresh spinach (not frozen)	675 grams
2 cups	fresh green onions, finely chopped	500 grams
2 cloves	crushed garlic	
2 tsp	Hungarian paprika	10 mL
2 tsp	dry oregano flakes	10 mL
2 tsp	fresh ground black pepper	10 mL
2 tsp	salt (optional)	10 mL
2 cups	stewed tomatoes, finely chopped or puréed	500 mL

Method:

1. Thoroughly wash stewing lamb and remove excess fat. Cover the lamb with cold water and bring to a boil. Reduce the heat to medium and continue to cook for approximately 1 ¹/₂ to 2 hours or until the meat is very tender. Remove from heat, cool and retain liquid.

2. Wash fresh spinach thoroughly and chop into small pieces. In a heavy skillet containing 2 tbsp extra virgin olive oil, add paprika, spices, green onions and garlic. Sauté for about three minutes over medium heat. Add chopped spinach and chopped or puréed tomatoes.

3. In a deep casserole dish, place cooked lamb. Add the sautéed spinach and tomato mixture. Strain and add about 1 ¹/₂ cups of the liquid the lamb was boiled in. Stir to blend all the ingredients. Bake uncovered in a hot oven of 375° F or 190° C oven for approximately 1 hour or until the meat has browned and most of the liquid is absorbed.

4. This delicious casserole is often served with rice or roast potatoes and is always served with cold, plain yoghurt.

RICE PILAF

Perhaps one of the most traditionally Greek dishes is Rice pilaf. There are endless varieties of pilaf. What pilaf actually means is rice cooked in a way that absorbs the flavor of the juice, stock or sauce in which it is cooked. It is important to keep in mind that the ratio of liquid to rice is about four to one, four cups of liquid to one cup of uncooked rice. The ratio may vary slightly if there are additional ingredients in the pilaf such as vegetables. Often the cooked chicken, lamb, beef or fish is placed in the casserole dish, together with the stock in which the meat was boiled. The sautéed rice is then added to the casserole dish and arranged around the meat. The liquid is absorbed by the rice during the cooking process which takes place in the oven. The result is the meat or fish together with its rice pilaf. This is the simple, traditional method which has been used for generations. The following recipes are just a few of the more common types of delicious Greek rice pilaf.

CHICKEN RICE PILAF

1/4 cup	onion, chopped finely	60 mL
1/4 cup	celery hearts, finely chopped	60 mL
2 tbsp	melted butter or olive oil	30 mL
1/2 tsp	fresh ground black pepper	3 mL
3/4 cup	uncooked rice	80 mL
1 clove	crushed garlic	
3 cups	chicken stock	750 mL

RED CHICKEN RICE PILAF

1/4 cup	onion, chopped finely	60 mL
1/4 cup	celery hearts, finely chopped	60 mL
2 tbsp	melted butter or olive oil	30 mL
1/2 tsp	fresh ground black pepper	3 mL
2 tsp	Hungarian paprika	10 mL
1 clove	crushed garlic	
1/2 cup	stewed tomatoes, puréed	125 mL
3/4 cup	uncooked rice	80 mL
2 1/2 cups	chicken stock	625 mL

VEGETABLE WHITE RICE PILAF

1/4 cup	white or red onion, finely chopped	60 mL
1/4 cup	celery hearts, finely chopped	60 mL
2 tbsp	melted butter or olive oil	30 mL
1/4 cup	sweet red bell pepper, finely chopped	60 mL
1/4 cup	sweet green or yellow bell pepper, finely chopped	60 mL
2 cloves	crushed garlic	
1/2 tsp	fresh ground black pepper	3 mL
3/4 cup	uncooked rice	80 mL
2 1/2 cups	chicken, beef, lamb, vegetable or fish stock	625 mL

VEGETABLE RED RICE PILAF
(same recipe as above except add the following:)

2 tsp	Hungarian paprika	10 mL
1/4 cup	stewed tomatoes, finely chopped or puréed	60 mL

METHOD:

The methods for all of the rice pilaf are the same.

1. In a saucepan containing butter or olive oil, add the paprika where applicable. Add the crushed garlic and chopped vegetables. Salt and pepper to taste. Sauté over medium heat until the onions begin to get transparent. Add the tomatoes, again where required. Simmer for about two minutes until all ingredients are blended. Remove from heat.

2. Wash and drain the uncooked rice. Add the rice to the vegetable mixture and blend together with the vegetables. At this point, the uncooked rice and vegetable mixture is placed in a casserole dish, usually surrounding cooked meat, chicken or fish. Whatever meat or fish is being used is completely cooked before adding the rice. Strain and add about 1 litre or 4 cups of the stock the meat was cooked in. Bake the casserole in a hot oven, 375° F or 190° C for approximately 35 to 40 minutes or until the rice is soft and fluffy and has absorbed all of the liquid. The rice not only absorbed the liquid, but also the flavor of the meat. This is rice pilaf.

3. If you do not wish to include meat in your recipe, it may be omitted. The same flavor can be achieved by using the meat, chicken, fish or vegetable stock only.

GREEK STYLE CHILE

1 lb	lean ground beef or lamb	450 grams
1 cup	white onion, finely chopped	250 grams
1/2 cup	sweet green bell pepper, finely chopped	125 grams
1/2 cup	sweet red bell pepper, finely chopped	125 grams
2 cups	stewed tomatoes, chopped	500 grains
2 tbsp	olive oil	30 mL
2 cloves	crushed garlic	
2 tsp	Hungarian paprika	10 mL
1 tsp	fresh ground black pepper	5 mL
1 tsp	crushed chile pepper or cayenne powder	5 mL
1 tsp	salt (optional)	5 mL
3 cups	cooked red or brown kidney beans, canned may be used	750 mL
1/2 cup	cold water	125 mL

METHOD:

1. Brown the meat in a heavy saucepan containing olive oil. Add crushed garlic and onions and peppers. Add paprika and salt and pepper to taste. Sauté over medium heat until the onions begin to turn golden brown around the edges. Add the tomatoes and the kidney beans. Add the crushed chile pepper or cayenne powder last.

2. Stir all ingredients together until thoroughly blended. Add water and cook over low heat for about fifteen minutes, stirring often to prevent the bottom from sticking. The chile will thicken. Serve hot with crusty fresh Greek bread and a salad. Don't forget the olives and feta cheese!

GROUND LAMB MEAT LOAF WITH SAUTÉED PEPPER, TOMATO AND GARLIC SAUCE

2 lb	lean ground, local lamb	1 kg
1/2 cup	white onion, finely chopped	125 mL
1/4 cup	finely chopped fresh parsley	60 mL
1/3 cup	dry bread crumbs or 2 slices soaked bread	80 mL
1 tsp	fresh ground black pepper	5 mL
1 tsp	salt (optional)	5 mL
1 egg	well beaten	

Topping

2 1/2 cups	white potatoes, chopped	750 mL
1 1/2 cups	fresh carrots, chopped	375 mL
2 tbsp	sour cream or tzatziki	30 mL
1 tbsp	butter	15 mL
1/4 cup	milk	
1 tsp	salt (optional)	5 mL

Sauce

1 1/2 cups	sweet, red bell peppers, finely chopped	375 mL
4 cloves	crushed garlic	
2 tbsp	extra virgin olive oil	39 mL
1 1/2 cups	stewed tomatoes	375 mL

METHOD:

1. Combine ground lamb, chopped onions, parsley, black pepper and salt in a large bowl. Add bread crumbs or sliced bread. (If using the bread, soak it in cold water and immediately squeeze all of the moisture out by hand. Soaked bread adds moistness to the meat loaf). Add beaten egg. Combine all ingredients well, by hand, and form into a loaf shape. Place in a greased, shallow casserole dish.

Bake at 375° F or 190° C for approximately one hour or until the juices run clear when the meat is punctured.

2. Bring potatoes and carrots to a boil and simmer over medium heat until soft. Drain the cooked potatoes and carrots and place in a bowl. Add sour cream or tzatziki, butter and milk. Add salt to taste. Mash by hand or using an electric beater until smooth and fluffy. Heap the mashed potatoes and carrots over the cooked meat loaf, creating a peak design. Place under broiler for about five minutes or until golden brown.

3. In a skillet containing olive oil, add chopped peppers, and garlic. Sauté over moderate heat until the peppers and garlic have turned golden brown around the edges. Reduce the heat and add stewed tomatoes. Simmer together for about 5 minutes. Remove from heat and cool slightly before serving with meat loaf. The sauce may be puréed, if preferred. Serve hot from the oven.

TRADITIONAL BAKED MACARONI AND GROUND BEEF CASSEROLE

1 lb	pasta (elbows work well)	450 grams
1 1/2 lb	extra lean ground beef	675 grams
1/2 cup	white onion, finely chopped	125 mL
2 tbsp	extra virgin olive oil	30 mL
2 cloves	crushed garlic	
4 tbsp	tomato paste	60 mL
1 cup	cold water	250 mL
3/4 cup	dry red wine	160 mL
1 tsp	fresh ground allspice powder	5 mL
1 tsp	fresh ground nutmeg	5 mL
1/2 tsp	fresh ground cinnamon	3 mL
1/3 cup	dry, unseasoned bread crumbs	80 mL
1/3 cup	melted butter	80 mL
5 cups	milk	1 litre + 250 mL
6	eggs, well beaten	
1 1/2 cup	fresh grated parmesan or romano cheese	375 mL

METHOD:

1. Sauté the onion in olive oil until golden brown. Add the meat and cook until browned. Add crushed garlic and spices. Add tomato paste, water and wine. Simmer for about five minutes. Remove from heat and cool. Boil the pasta in water until cooked and drain. Add melted butter to cooked pasta. Add one cup of the grated cheese and toss until blended.

2. Butter a large rectangular baking dish (a glass dish works well). Sprinkle half of the bread crumbs on the bottom of the dish. Pour half of the pasta over the bread crumbs. Pour all of the meat mixture over the bottom layer of pasta, and top with the remaining pasta. Sprinkle the top with the remainder of the bread crumbs.

3. Beat the eggs until they are very light and foamy. Add the milk and continue beating until they are completely blended. Pour the egg and milk mixture over the top of the casserole and sprinkle with the remaining grated cheese. More cheese may be used if desired. Bake at 375 degree F or 190° C for approximately 45 minutes or until golden brown and fluffy. Serve with a leafy salad for a delicious and hearty meal.

STUFFED BELL PEPPERS WITH GROUND BEEF, NUTTY RICE

6	sweet bell peppers, red, green and yellow	
1 lb	lean ground beef (lamb or pork may be substituted)	450 grams
1 1/2 cups	uncooked, short grain rice	375 mL
1/4 cup	toasted pine seeds	60 mL
1/2 cup	white onion, finely chopped	125 mL
4 tbsp	extra virgin olive oil	60 mL
3 cloves	crushed garlic	
1 tsp	fresh ground black pepper	5 mL
1 tsp	salt (optional)	5 mL
2 1/2 cups	stewed tomatoes, puréed	625 mL
1/3 cup	fresh parsley leaves, finely chopped	80 mL
1 1/2 cups	light chicken stock or water	375 mL

METHOD:

1. Thoroughly wash peppers, and using a sharp knife, cut a small circle around the stem, at the top of each pepper. Remove the stem and the circle, ensuring not to split the pepper. The opening of the pepper should be about 1 1/2 in. or 4 cm. in diameter. Remove the seeds and veins from the inside of the pepper and discard, together with the stem. Wash the inside and leave about 1 tsp of water at the bottom of each pepper. Place in a deep, rectangular baking dish.

2. Boil the rice for approximately 3 minutes or until it just begins to soften. Remove from heat and drain from water. In a large saucepan containing 2 tbsp of olive oil, sauté the ground meat. When the meat is almost browned, add the chopped onion and 2 cloves of garlic. Add oregano and salt and pepper. Continue to sauté over medium heat until the onions become transparent. Sauté pine seeds in a non-stick pan containing 1 tbsp butter until deep golden brown in color. Add toasted pine seeds and butter to the meat and onion mixture.

3. Add the partially cooked rice and the chopped parsley to the meat and blend all ingredients together. Carefully, stuff about 6 tbsp or 90 mL of meat and rice filling into each pepper, pack the stuffing fairly tightly.

4. Place 2 ¹/2 cups of puréed, stewed tomatoes in a large saucepan. Add 1 clove of crushed garlic and 1 ¹/2 cups of stock or water. Add 2 tbsp of extra virgin olive oil and mixture to a boil. Remove from heat and add to the stuffed peppers. The liquid should be carefully poured around the peppers. No liquid should be poured over the stuffed peppers. The rice mixture must remain dry. Cover tightly with aluminum foil and bake at 400° F or 225° C for approximately 1 ¹/2 hours. Remove foil. Rice should be fluffy and peppers should be soft. Serve hot. Stuffed peppers may be accompanied by any eggplant dish or salad. Don't forget the crusty bread and olives.

MARINATED BABY LAMB CHOPS

Marinade

¹/4 cup	extra virgin olive oil	60 mL
2 cloves	crushed garlic	
¹/4 cup	fresh squeezed lemon juice (not bottled)	60 mL
2 tsp	dry oregano flakes, or	10 mL
1 tbsp	fresh oregano, finely chopped	15 mL
1 tbsp	fresh chopped mint	15 mL
1 tsp	fresh ground black pepper	5 mL
1 tsp	salt (optional)	5 mL

METHOD:

1. Thoroughly wash and dry the lamb chops. Place in a shallow, glass baking dish and cover with marinade. Cover tightly with plastic wrap and refrigerate for at least eight hours.

2. Remove the chops from the marinade and grill or barbecue until tender. Serve with vegetable rice pilaf (recipe follows) and fried eggplant with garlic and lemon. Don't forget the feta cheese and black olives!

MOUSSAKA WITH GROUND BEEF, SLICED POTATOES AND EGGPLANT

2	large eggplants	
1 1/2 lb	lean ground beef or fresh lamb	675 grams
4 tbsp	extra virgin olive oil	60 mL
1 cup	white onion, finely chopped	250 mL
2 cloves	crushed garlic	
1 1/2 cups	tomato sauce or puréed stewed tomatoes	375 mL
1/3 cup	fresh parsley leaves, finely chopped	80 mL
6	large, white potatoes, peeled and sliced	
2	whole eggs, well beaten	
1/2 cup	dry, unseasoned bread crumbs	125 mL
3/4 cup	fresh grated parmesan or Romano, cheese	180 mL
1 tsp	fresh ground black pepper	5 mL
1 tsp	fresh ground cinnamon powder	5 mL
1 tsp	fresh ground allspice powder	5 mL
1 tsp	fresh ground nutmeg	5 mL
1 tsp	salt (optional)	5 mL

Béchamel sauce for topping (recipe follows)

METHOD:

1. Thoroughly wash and dry eggplants and slice in 1/4 in. or 1 cm. thickness. Do not peel the eggplant. Brush the slices with olive oil and brown in a non-stick pan until golden brown on both sides. Eggplant should be only slightly softened. Set aside to cool.

2. Sauté meat, onion and crushed garlic in a hot skillet containing about 1 tbsp olive oil, until the meat is browned and the onion is transparent. Add spices, chopped parsley and tomato sauce. Cook over moderate heat until the tomato sauce is almost absorbed. Remove from heat and cool to room temperature. Add beaten eggs and half of the bread crumbs to the cooled meat mixture.

3. In a greased, rectangular casserole dish approximately 12 in. x 14 in. x 3 in. or

30 cm. x 35 cm. x 7.5 cm., spread the remainder of the bread crumbs evenly over the bottom of the baking dish. Peel and slice raw potatoes to $1/4$ in. or 1 cm. thickness. Alternate layers of eggplant, sliced potatoes and meat mixture. Begin with the potatoes and end with the eggplant. Top with fresh grated cheese.

4. Pour Béchamel sauce evenly over the top of the casserole and bake at 400° F or 200° C for approximately one hour. Allow the Moussaka to cool slightly before serving. This will help it to keep its shape when serving. Serve with fresh bread, Greek salad and calamata olives. Tasty!

BÉCHAMEL SAUCE FOR MOUSSAKA

5 tbsp	butter	75 mL
5 tbsp	white flour	75 mL
4 cups	milk	1 litre
4	egg yolks, well beaten	
$1/2$ tsp	fresh ground nutmeg	3 mL
$1/2$ tsp	salt (optional)	3 mL
$1/2$ tsp	fresh ground black pepper	3 mL
$1/4$ cup	grated, fresh parmesan cheese (Romano cheese may be used)	60 mL

METHOD:

1. Melt butter in the top of a double boiler. Add the flour and stir constantly, using a wire whisk until well blended. Gradually add milk, continuing to constantly stir with the whisk. Cook and stir over high heat until the mixture thickens and becomes very smooth.

2. In a separate bowl, beat the egg yolks until foamy. Add a small amount of the milk mixture, about a $1/2$ cup. Continue to beat until the eggs and the milk mixture are well blended. Add to the rest of the milk mixture, stirring constantly, still using the wire whisk. Gradually add the grated cheese and blend together. The wire whisk prevents the mixture from becoming lumpy during cooking.

3. Pour over the prepared Moussaka.

BAKED LAMB STEW WITH ORZO AND SWEET RED AND YELLOW PEPPERS

(Orzo is a rice-shaped pasta)

2 lb	lean stewing lamb	900 grams
3 cups	cold water (vegetable stock may be used)	750 mL
1 cup	white onion, chopped	250 mL
1 cup	sweet red bell pepper, chopped	250 mL
1/2 cup	sweet yellow bell pepper, chopped	125 mL
1/2 cup	celery hearts, chopped	125 mL
2 cloves	crushed garlic	
4 tbsp	extra virgin olive oil	60 mL
1/4 cup	fresh oregano leaves, finely chopped	60 mL
1 tsp	dry basil	5 mL
1 1/2 tsp	fresh ground black pepper	8 mL
1/2 tsp	salt (optional)	3 mL
2 tsp	Hungarian paprika	10 mL
1 1/2 cups	stewed tomatoes, chopped or puréed	
6 cups	liquid (water or stock)	1 1/2 litres
1 1/2 cups	uncooked orzo	375 mL

Ratio: 1 cup or 250 mL of orzo to 4 cups or 1 litre of liquid (approx. measurements)

METHOD:

1. Wash lamb meat thoroughly in cold water and cut into cubes. Place meat in a deep saucepan and cover with 3 cups of water or stock. Cover and simmer over moderate heat for approximately 1 1/2 hours or until meat is tender. Retain the liquid.

2. In a large saucepan, add oil, salt and pepper, chopped onion and garlic and basil. Remove the cooked lamb from the liquid and add to the chopped onion and spaces. Sauté for approximately five minutes over high heat until the meat begins to brown and the onions begin to caramelize. Add the chopped peppers and fresh oregano. Continue cooking for an additional 3 minutes. Add the uncooked orzo and blend all ingredients.

3. Transfer the lamb and sautéed vegetables into a rectangular casserole dish about 12 in. x 14 in. or 30 cm. x 35 cm. A glass or ceramic dish works well. Add the lamb stock from the boiling process to the puréed stewed tomatoes. Add enough water or additional stock to make 6 cups of liquid. Pour liquid over the lamb and vegetables and stir to blend ingredients together. Bake at 400° F or 200° C for approximately 35 minutes or until all the liquid has been absorbed and the orzo is soft and fluffy. If the orzo is not soft, add more liquid, approximately 1 cup or 250 mL at a time and continue cooking. Serve immediately with fresh bread and a salad. A hearty and delicious dish.

This recipe may also be made with chicken or beef and using chicken or beef stock in place of vegetable stock or water.

CHICKEN AND EGGPLANT PTARMIGAN WITH PORTOBELLO MUSHROOMS

3	small, boneless chicken breasts, cut in half	
1	small eggplant	
2 cups	Portobello mushrooms	500 mL
2 cloves	crushed garlic	
1 cup	coarsely grated mozzarella cheese	250 mL
1 cup	coarsely grated parmesan cheese	250 mL
1/4 cup	extra virgin olive oil	60 mL
2 tsp	dry oregano flakes	10 mL
1 tsp	fresh ground black pepper	5 mL
1 tsp	dry basil	5 mL
2	whole eggs, well beaten	
1/2 cup	milk	125 mL
1 1/2 cups	unseasoned, dry bread crumbs for dredging	375 mL

Sauce

2 1/2 cups	stewed tomatoes, puréed	625 mL
2 tbsp	extra virgin olive oil	30 mL
1 tsp	dry oregano flakes	5 mL
1/2 tsp	dry basil	3 mL
1 tsp	salt (optional)	5 mL
2 cloves	crushed garlic	
1/2 cup	chicken stock	125 mL

METHOD:

1. Wash chicken breasts and cut in half to make 6 pieces. Pound with a steel mallet to 1/4 in. or 1 cm. thickness. Combine bread crumbs with 2 tsp oregano flakes, 1 tsp basil and 1 tsp black pepper. In a small bowl combine milk and eggs and

beat until light and fluffy. Dip the chicken pieces in the egg and milk mixture and dredge in bread crumbs. Sauté in a non-stick pan, containing 2 tbsp olive oil until golden brown. Do not overcook. Remove and place cooked chicken breast fillets in a rectangular, oiled casserole dish.

2. Wash and slice eggplant into $1/4$ in. or 1 cm. thick slices. Brush with olive oil and brown in a non-stick pan over moderate heat until golden brown. Eggplant should be slightly softened, not mushy. Do not peel. Place one slice of cooked eggplant on each chicken fillet in the casserole dish. Brush to clean, and slice the mushrooms. Brown in a non-stick pan containing 1 tbsp olive oil. Divide the mushroom evenly, placing them on top of each slice of eggplant. Sprinkle with mozzarella and parmesan cheeses.

3. In a saucepan containing 2 tbsp extra virgin olive oil, add puréed tomatoes, crushed garlic, oregano and basil. Add chicken stock and simmer over medium heat for approximately 5 minutes. Spoon approximately 1 $1/4$ cups of sauce around the chicken pieces. Bake, uncovered at 400° F or 200° C for approximately 15 minutes until the cheeses melt. Add the remainder of sauce to 3 cups cooked pasta, toss and serve with chicken.

CHICKEN BREASTS
WITH SPICY RED ONION SAUCE

2	large, chicken breasts, cut in half to make 4 pieces (boneless breasts may be used)	
4 cups	chicken stock	1 litre
2 cups	red onions, cut in thin wedge shapes or slivers	500 mL
1/2 cup	celery hearts, chopped finely	125 mL
1/2 cup	sweet red bell pepper, cut in slivers	125 mL
1/2 cup	sweet yellow bell pepper, cut in slivers	125 mL
2 cloves	crushed garlic	
1/2 tsp	fresh ground black peppers	3 mL
1/2 tsp	salt (optional)	3 mL
2 tsp	Hungarian paprika	10 mL
1 1/2 cups	stewed tomatoes, puréed or chopped finely	375 mL
2 tbsp	extra virgin olive oil	30 mL
1/2 tsp	cayenne pepper powder or crushed chile peppers	3 mL

METHOD:

1. Thoroughly wash chicken breasts and cut in half to make 4 pieces. Discard the skin and place chicken in a large saucepan. Add chicken stock. Cover and bring to a boil. Simmer over medium heat for about 1 1/2 hours or until they are very tender. Remove from heat.

2. In a large saucepan containing olive oil, add paprika, crushed garlic and onions. Sauté over medium heat until the onions caramelize and turn golden brown. Add the celery and peppers and continue to sauté for an additional 3 - 5 minutes, just until the celery softens. Add tomatoes and simmer for about one minute.

3. Place the cooked chicken breasts in a casserole dish and pour onion sauce over the chicken. Strain the remainder of the chicken stock that is left after boiling the chicken breasts and add to the casserole. There should be about one cup of stock left. Bake uncovered at 400° F or 200° C for approximately 45 minutes. The sauce will reduce and thicken during the cooking time. The casserole should have a golden brown color on the top when it is done. Remove from oven and serve with white or brown rice or fluffy mashed potatoes.

BAKED CHICKEN BREASTS WITH CRUSHED WALNUTS AND RED WINE

1	whole 2 $^1/_2$ lb or 1 kg chicken, cut into pieces or 4 chicken breasts, cut in half	
$^2/_3$ cup	white flour	160 ml
1 tsp	Hungarian paprika	5 mL
$^1/_3$ cup	butter	80 mL
4 cloves	crushed garlic	
$^1/_4$ cup	fresh green onions, finely chopped (optional)	60 mL
$^1/_2$ cup	fresh parsley leaves, finely chopped	125 mL
$^1/_2$ cup	dry red wine (white wine may be used)	125 mL
1 tsp	fresh ground black pepper	5 mL
$^1/_2$ cup	finely chopped, shelled walnuts (not packaged)	125 mL
4 cups	chicken stock	1 litre

METHOD:

1. Wash and cut chicken into pieces or use chicken breasts, cut in half. Remove and discard the skin. Boil the chicken in chicken stock for about 1 $^1/_2$ hours or until very tender and completely cooked. Remove from heat.

2. In a non-stick saucepan, melt butter and add paprika. Add flour and crushed garlic. Sauté over low heat, stirring with a wire whisk until the flour and butter are blended and the flour begins to turn a golden brown color. Do not overcook or burn the flour. Add the onions (optional). Stir constantly with the wire whisk and add the chicken stock that remains after boiling the chicken. Add additional chicken stock to make up about 4 cups. Stir constantly with whisk over medium heat until the sauce thickens. Using the whisk to stir the sauce prevents any lumps from forming. Add the wine and chopped parsley. Continue to stir and thicken for about 1 minute. For a thicker sauce, use an additional 1 tbsp or 15 mL when adding the flour to the butter.

3. Place the cooked chicken pieces in a shallow casserole dish and cover with the sauce. Sprinkle with crushed walnuts and bake at 375° F or 175° C for approximately 45 minutes until the casserole begins to turn golden brown. Remove from the oven and serve hot. This dish may be served with white or brown rice or potatoes and any colorful salad.

SALTED COD FISH WITH SPICY RED RICE PILAF CASSEROLE

2 1/2 lb	boneless, skinless, salted cod fish	1 kg
2 1/2 cups	uncooked white rice	625 mL
2/3 cup	white onion, finely chopped	80 mL
2 tbsp	extra virgin olive oil	30 mL
3 tsp	Hungarian paprika	15 mL
1 clove	crushed garlic	
1 tsp	fresh ground black pepper	5 mL
1 tsp	cayenne powder or crushed hot chile peppers	5 mL
1 cup	stewed tomatoes, puréed or finely chopped	250 mL
4 cups	fish stock	1 litre

METHOD:

1. Place the cod fish in cold water and soak for at least 8 hours, to remove excess salt. Place the soaked, boneless cod in a saucepan and add about 4 1/2 cups or 1 litre of water. Bring to a boil and reduce heat. Simmer for about a 1/2 hour over medium heat until the fish is flaky. Remove from heat and cool.

2. In a large skillet containing olive oil, add paprika, chopped onions and garlic. Sauté until the onions are soft, do not brown. Add spices and tomatoes. Add the uncooked rice and blend all ingredients.

3. Place the cooked cod fish pieces in a casserole dish and cover with the rice and tomato mixture. Add the remainder of the fish stock the cod was cooked in. There should be about 4 cups. Cook at 400° F or 200° C for approximately 45 minutes or until the rice has absorbed all of the liquid and is soft and fluffy. Remove from oven. This dish may be served hot or cold and makes a delicious and very original appetizer. As a meal on its own, add fresh bread and a salad.

EASY AND DELICIOUS MEATBALL AND POTATO CASSEROLE

1 ¹/₂ lb	fresh ground lean beef or lamb	675 grams
¹/₂ cup	fresh parsley, finely chopped	125 mL
¹/₂ cup	white onion, finely chopped	125 mL
¹/₄ cup	toasted pine nuts	60 mL
1 tsp	fresh ground allspice	5 mL
1 tsp	fresh ground cinnamon powder	5 mL
1 tsp	fresh ground black pepper	5 mL
1 tsp	salt (optional)	5 mL
2 tbsp	extra virgin olive oil	15 mL
6	large white potatoes, peeled and cut	
¹/₂ cup	beef stock	125 mL
3 cups	stewed tomatoes, puréed	750 mL
1 tsp	Hungarian paprika	5 mL

METHOD:

1. Combine ground meat, chopped onion, chopped parsley and spices in a large bowl. Pan toast pine nuts in 1 tbsp butter, cool, place in a food processor and chop. Add chopped nuts to the meat mixture. Combine all ingredients and shape into oval meatballs about the size of limes. Arrange in a large rectangular casserole dish.

2. Wash and peel potatoes and cut into wedges. Arrange in the pan together with the meatballs. Sprinkle with olive oil and garnish with paprika. Place under the broiler for about a ¹/₂ hour and brown the meat and potatoes. Check regularly to prevent burning. Turn the potatoes and meat to ensure they become browned on all sides. Remove from oven. Combine tomatoes and beef stock and pour over casserole. Place back in the oven and bake at 400° F or 200° C for approximately 45 minutes or until the potatoes are fork tender. Serve hot. Add any vegetables as an accompaniment and this dish will become a family favorite.

TENDER PORK SPARE RIBS AND KIDNEY BEAN STEW

3 lb	pork back ribs or baby back ribs	1 1/2 kg
1 1/2 cups	cooked, white kidney beans, and	325 mL
1 1/2 cups	cooked, red kidney beans (canned work well)	325 mL
1 cup	stewed tomatoes, chopped or puréed	250 mL
1/2 cup	white onion, finely chopped	125 mL
1/2 cup	sweet bell pepper, red or green, chopped	125 mL
1/2 cup	celery hearts, finely chopped	
6 cups	beef stock	1 1/2 litres
2 tsp	Hungarian paprika	10 mL
1 tsp	fresh ground black pepper	5 mL
2 cloves	crushed garlic	
2 tbsp	extra virgin olive oil	15 mL
1 tsp	dry oregano flakes	5 mL
1/4 cup	chopped parsley leaves	60 mL

METHOD:

1. Separate spare ribs into serving portion pieces and cook in beef stock. Remove and discard any excess fat from the ribs before cooking. Wash thoroughly and simmer over medium heat for approximately 2 hours or until very tender. Remove from heat.

2. In a heavy skillet containing olive oil, add all the vegetables and spices. Sauté over moderately high heat for about five minutes until the onion starts to turn golden brown. Add tomatoes and parsley. Add kidney beans and blend all ingredients together. Place the cooked ribs in an open baking dish and add the vegetables and kidney bean mixture. Strain the liquid remaining from the boiling process of the spare ribs and pour over casserole. There should be about 2 cups of liquid remaining. Stir until all ingredients are combined.

3. Bake at 400° F or 200° C for approximately 45 minutes or until the liquid thickens and the casserole begins to brown. Most of the liquid will be absorbed. Serve hot from the oven. This is a hearty and flavorful meal which is served as a main dish. Fresh bread and a crisp salad make it complete.

COLORFUL CHICKEN AND RICE PILAF

1 - 2 1/2 lb whole chicken		1 kg
2 tbsp	olive oil	30 mL
1/2 cup	white onion, finely chopped	125 mL
1/4 cup	celery hearts, finely chopped	60 mL
1/4 cup	sweet green bell pepper, chopped	60 mL
1 cup	mushrooms, sliced or chopped	250 mL
6 cups	chicken stock	1 1/2 litre
2 cloves	crushed garlic	
1/2 tsp	fresh ground black pepper	3 mL
1/2 tsp	salt (optional)	3 mL
2 cups	white rice	500 mL

METHOD:

1. Thoroughly wash and dry chicken and cut into pieces. Remove and discard the skin and place in a large saucepan. Add chicken stock and bring to a boil. Cover and simmer over medium heat for about 1 1/2 hours or until very tender. Remove from heat and set aside.

2. In a saucepan containing olive oil, add crushed garlic, chopped onions, celery and peppers. Sauté over medium heat for about 5 minutes or until the onions become transparent. Add salt and pepper and uncooked rice. Combine all ingredients.

2. Place cooked chicken pieces in a casserole dish and surround with the rice and vegetable mixture. Strain the remaining chicken stock used to boil the chicken into the casserole. There should be about 2 cups left. Add additional chicken stock to make up about 6 cups. Bake at 375° F or 175 or 190° C for about 35 minutes or until the liquid has been absorbed and the rice is fluffy and soft. Test the rice, if not cooked add more stock one cup at a time and continue to cook until soft. Remove from oven and serve hot.

Note: To make red rice pilaf, add 2 tsp or 10 mL of Hungarian paprika to the olive oil when sautéing the vegetables and add 1/2 cup puréed, stewed tomatoes to the stock before baking.

BAKED LAMB AND FRESH OKRA STEW

2 ¹/₂ lb	lean stewing lamb	1 kg
6 cups	cold water	1 ¹/₂ litres
2 ¹/₂ lb	whole, fresh okra (not frozen)	1 kg
1 cup	white onion, chopped	250 mL
2 cups	stewed tomatoes, finely chopped	500 mL
2 cloves	crushed garlic	
1 tsp	fresh ground black pepper	5 mL
1 tsp	salt (optional)	5 mL
2 tsp	Hungarian paprika	10 mL
2 tbsp	extra virgin olive oil	30 mL

METHOD:

1. Wash lamb meat in cold water. Place in a deep saucepan and cover with about 6 cups of cold water (vegetable stock may be substituted). Cover and bring to a boil. Simmer over medium heat for about 1 ¹/₂ hours or until the lamb is very tender.

2. In a skillet containing olive oil, add crushed garlic, onions, paprika and salt and pepper. Sauté all ingredients over medium heat until the onions become caramelized and begin to turn golden brown around the edges.

3. Thoroughly wash the fresh okra. Cut off the stems but keep intact. Do not puncture the wall of the okra. Add the washed, fresh okra to the onion mixture. Combine all ingredients and add the tomatoes.

4. Place the cooked lamb pieces in a casserole dish and surround with the okra and tomato mixture. Strain the remaining stock from the boiling process of the lamb. There should be about 2 cups. Add an additional 2 cups of water or vegetable stock. Bake at 400° F or 200° C for approximately 1 hour or until the meat is very tender and most of the liquid has been absorbed. Remove from oven and serve hot with rice or potatoes. It may also be served on its own, accompanied by a fresh tabouli salad. Don't forget the toasted pita bread and calamata olives.

TRADITIONAL SHORT RIBS OF BEEF WITH VEGETABLES

2 1/2 lb	beef short ribs	1 kg
6 cups	beef stock	1 1/2 litres
1 cup	white onion, chopped	250 mL
1 1/2 cups	fresh carrots, sliced thickly	375 mL
1/2 cup	celery hearts, chopped coarsely	125 mL
3/4 cup	fresh or frozen, uncooked peas	180 mL
3 cups	potatoes, chopped coarsely	750 mL
2 cloves	crushed garlic	
1 tsp	fresh ground black pepper	5 mL
1 tsp	salt (optional)	5 mL
1/2 tsp	fresh ground allspice powder	3 mL
2 tbs	extra virgin olive oil	15 mL
2 tbsp	flour	15 mL
1 tbsp	butter	15 mL

METHOD:

1. Wash short ribs and place in a deep saucepan. Add beef stock and bring to a boil. Reduce heat, cover and simmer over medium heat for about 1 1/2 hours or until the meat is tender.

2. In a non-stick skillet containing 2 tbsp olive oil, sauté chopped onions, crushed garlic and celery until the onions become transparent. Brown the cooked short ribs in the pan with the vegetables. Add spices, carrots and potatoes. Continue to sauté over medium heat until the potatoes become browned and the onions caramelize. Add the peas and combine all the ingredients.

3. Transfer the meat and vegetables into a deep casserole dish. In a separate saucepan containing 1 tbsp melted butter, add the flour and stir with a wire whisk until the flour becomes golden brown in color. Strain the remaining stock from the short ribs into the flour and butter. There should be about 2 cups left. Add an additional 2 cups of beef stock to make a total of about 4 cups. Add this

liquid to the meat and vegetables. Cover and cook at 400° F or 200° C for approximately 1 hour or until the sauce has thickened and the meat and vegetables are tender. This meat and vegetable dish is a complete meal on its own when served with fresh bread. Of course you could always include feta cheese and calamata olives.

CABBAGE ROLLS WITH LEAN GROUND MEAT AND WHITE RICE IN SAVORY TOMATO SAUCE

1	large green cabbage	
1 1/2 lb	extra lean fresh ground beef or pork	675 grams
2 1/2 cups	uncooked white rice, parboiled	625 mL
3/4 cup	white onion, finely chopped	180 mL
1/2 cup	fresh parsley, finely chopped	125 mL
2 tsp	dry oregano flakes	10 mL
1 clove	crushed garlic	
1 tsp	fresh ground black pepper	5 mL
1 tsp	salt (optional)	5 mL

SAVORY TOMATO SAUCE

3 cups	stewed tomatoes, puréed	750 mL
1 cup	vegetable, chicken or light beef stock	250 mL
2 cloves	crushed garlic	
4 tbsp	extra virgin olive oil	60 mL
1/2 tsp	dry oregano flakes	3 mL
1/2 tsp	fresh ground black pepper	3 mL

METHOD:

1. Cut a deep circle, using a sharp knife, around the core of the cabbage and remove and discard it. Place the cabbage in a deep pot containing a small amount of boiling water, cover the pot tightly and allow the steam to separate the leaves. This steaming will also slightly soften the cabbage before the stuffing process. This is important as it allows flexibility and prevents the leaves from splitting or breaking. Remove the leaves from the pot one at a time and allow them to cool.

2. Parboil the rice for about 3 minutes until it is beginning to soften. Drain the water and set aside to cool. In a large bowl, combine parboiled rice, raw meat, chopped parsley and onions, 1 clove of crushed garlic and spices. Mix well using your hand, until all ingredients are combined. The mixture should stick together when squeezed.

3. Lay out one cabbage leaf at a time, stem portion toward you. Place about 4 tbsp or 60 mL of the rice and meat mixture at the bottom of the leaf. Roll the leaf away from you, tucking the sides in tightly. The finished roll should be tight and should not be falling apart. Place the cabbage roll, open end down, in a large, lightly oiled baking dish. Make sure the rolls are tightly pressed together. Continue this process until all of the leaves and stuffing is used.

4. Combine all the ingredients for the sauce in and mix together well. Cover the cabbage rolls with sauce. Bake at 375° F or 190° C, tightly covered for about one hour. Remove the cover and add more sauce if necessary. Continue baking for another half hour or until the rice is soft and the cabbage is golden brown. Remove from the oven and serve immediately.

POT ROAST OF BEEF

1-3 $^1/_2$ - 4 lb roast of beef, any roast with a bone works well about 1 $^1/_2$ kg

12 small	potatoes	
2 cups	coarsely slices fresh carrots	500 mL
1 cup	coarsely chopped celery hearts	250 mL
1 cup	coarsely chopped turnip, peeled (optional)	250 mL
12 small	whole onions	
1 $^1/_2$ tsp	fresh ground black pepper	8 mL
1 $^1/_2$ tsp	salt (optional)	8 mL
2 tsp	fresh ground allspice powder	10 mL
2 tsp	Hungarian paprika	10 mL
2 cloves	crushed garlic	
2 tbsp	extra virgin olive oil	10 mL
3 tbsp	melted butter	45 mL
3 tbsp	white flour	45 mL
4 cups	beef stock	1 litre

METHOD:

1. Thoroughly wash the roast and place it in a deep, covered roasting pen. A heavy, ceramic covered iron roasting pan, heavy stainless steel or glass pan works well. Combine crushed garlic and olive oil and half of the spices. Rub the meat on all sides with this mixture. Allow the meat to marinate overnight. Add about 3 cups of beef stock to the bottom of the pan, cover tightly and slow roast at 375° F for 2 $^1/_2$ to 3 hours. Remove the lid and add all of the raw vegetables. Sprinkle the remainder of the spices, evenly over the raw vegetables. Cover and continue roasting for about 1 hour. At this point, most of the liquid will have been absorbed.

2. In a deep saucepan containing melted butter, add the flour and stir with a wire whisk until the flour begins to brown. Add about 3 cups or 750 mL more beef stock, slowly, while continually whisking until the gravy is smooth and begins to thicken. Add this gravy to the liquid remaining in the roast (there should be approximately one cup left, making a total of 4 cups or 1 litre of gravy). Uncover and continue cooking for about $^1/_2$ hour. Meat should be tender and juicy and vegetables should be soft. Serve this delicious meal with roasted peppers, feta cheese and crusty Greek bread

BAKED SOLE FILLETS
WITH VEGETABLE MEDLEY SAUCE

3 lb	sole fillets (any type of deep cold water fish fillets may be used, as well as any type of shellfish)	1 1/4 kg
2 cups	fresh green onions, finely chopped	500 mL
1/2 cup	celery hearts, finely chopped	125 mL
1/2 cup	sweet, red bell peppers, finely chopped	125 mL
1/2 cup	sweet, yellow bell peppers, finely chopped	125 mL
1/4 cup	fresh parsley leaves, finely chopped	60 mL
3 cups	stewed tomatoes, puréed or finely chopped	750 mL
3 tbsp	extra virgin olive oil	45 mL
4 cloves	crushed garlic	
2 tsp	dry oregano leaves	10 mL
1 tsp	fresh ground black pepper	5 mL
2 tbsp	fresh squeezed lemon juice (not bottled)	30 mL
	lemon slices or wedges for garnish	

METHOD:

1. Wash and arrange deboned, skinless fillets of fish in a baking dish. Squeeze fresh lemon directly over the fillets.

2. In a large non-stick saucepan, combine crushed garlic, chopped vegetables and spices in 3 tbsp olive oil. Sauté over medium heat until the vegetables begin to soften. Add the tomatoes. Pour the sautéed vegetables carefully over and around the uncooked fish fillets. Bake at 400° F or 200° C for approximately 20 minutes or until the fish is flaky. Do not overcook. Some of the sauce will be absorbed.

3. Place fish fillets on a serving platter and surround with the sauce. Garnish with fresh lemon wedges or slices. This dish may be served hot or cold. If served hot, include fluffy mashed potatoes, roast potatoes or rice and don't forget the toasted pita bread wedges.

SUCCULENT ROASTED PORK TENDERLOIN WITH FRESH LEEKS AND PRUNES

1-3 - 3 $^{1}/_{2}$ lb pork tenderloin roast		about 1 $^{1}/_{4}$ kg
2 cups	fresh leeks, finely chopped	500 mL
2 cups	pitted prunes, whole or cut in half	500 mL
2 cups	sweet apples, cut in wedges, core removed	500 mL
2 cloves	crushed garlic	
2 tsp	Hungarian paprika	10 mL
2 tbsp	extra virgin olive oil	30 mL
2 cups	chicken or vegetable stock	500 mL
1 tsp	fresh ground black pepper	5 mL

Marinade for Tenderloin

$^{1}/_{4}$ cup	olive oil	60 mL
2 cloves	crushed garlic	
2 tbsp	dark brown sugar	30 mL
1 tsp	fresh ground black pepper	5 mL
$^{1}/_{4}$ cup	apple juice or apple cider	60 mL

METHOD:

1. Combine all ingredients of marinade and pour over pork tenderloin. Turn the meat in the marinade to ensure that the whole roast is coated. Cover tightly and refrigerate for at least eight hours.

2. In a large saucepan containing 2 tbsp extra virgin olive oil, add chopped leeks, paprika, black pepper and crushed garlic. Sauté over medium heat until the leeks begin to turn golden brown. Add dried prunes and apple wedges. Remove from heat and blend all ingredients. Add chicken or vegetable stock.

3. Place the marinated meat in a roasting pan. Pour the remaining marinade over the roast and place under the broiler, turning regularly until the meat is golden brown. The browning process should take about 35 to 45 minutes. When the

meat is browned, surround the roast with the leek/prune and apple mixture. Continue to cook, uncovered at 400° F or 200° C for about 1 hour or until the pork is cooked. Use a meat thermometer to test the meat. Most of the liquid will have evaporated and the prunes will be very soft.

4. Remove from the oven and slice the roast. Place on a platter and gently add the sauce around the meat slices. Serve with roast potatoes or plain white rice. A delicious taste experience!

GREEK MEAT BALLS IN TOMATO SAUCE

2 lb	extra lean ground beef or lamb	1 kg
3 slices	white or whole wheat bread	
2 tsp	fresh ground black pepper	10 mL
1 tsp	salt (optional)	5 mL
2 cloves	fresh crushed garlic	
3/4 cup	white onion, very finely chopped	80 mL
2	whole eggs, beaten	
1/2 cup	fresh mint leaves, very finely chopped	125 mL
1/2 cup	white flour	125 mL
2 tbsp	extra virgin olive oil (for frying meatballs)	30 mL

Sauce

2 1/2 cups	stewed tomatoes, puréed	750 mL
3 tbsp	extra virgin olive oil	45 mL
1/2 cup	beef or vegetable stock	125 mL
1 clove	crushed garlic	
1/2 tsp	fresh ground black pepper	3 mL
1 1/2 tsp	dry oregano flakes	8 mL

METHOD:

1. In a large bowl, combine meat, chopped onion, chopped mint, garlic, beaten eggs and spices. Soak bread in cold water and squeeze out by hand. Add to the meat mixture. Combine all ingredients well, by hand. Shape into meatballs and dredge on all sides in flour. Sauté in a non-stick pan containing 3 tbsp olive oil, over medium heat, turning frequently until meatballs are browned and the juices run clear. Remove from pan and place in a rectangular casserole dish.

2. Combine stewed tomatoes, 3 tbsp olive oil, stock, 1 clove crushed garlic, 1/2 tsp black pepper and oregano flakes. Pour over the meatballs in the casserole dish. Bake at 400° F or 200° C for approximately 35 - 45 minutes or until the meatballs become fluffy and the sauce has thickened. Remove from oven and serve immediately with fluffy mashed potatoes or white or brown rice. Add any salad and this meal will become a favorite. Don't forget the feta cheese!

SOUVLAKI! SOUVLAKI! SOUVLAKI!

This recipe may be made with lamb, chicken, pork or beef. Whichever type of meat is chosen, the marinade which creates the authentic Greek souvlaki flavor, is the same. In order to achieve perfect souvlaki, tender and juicy, be sure to use only fine quality cuts of meat, free from fat and veins.

Marinade

1/2 cup	extra virgin olive oil	125 mL
1/2 cup	fresh squeezed lemon juice (not bottled)	125 mL
2 cloves	crushed garlic	
4 tsp	dry oregano flakes	20 mL
2 tsp	dry mint flakes	10 mL
2 tsp	fresh ground black pepper	10 mL
1 tsp	salt	5 mL

METHOD:

1. Cut meat or chicken into cubes approximately 1 in. or 2 1/2 cm. in diameter. Place the meat cubes in a large bowl and cover with marinade. Cover tightly and refrigerate for at least eight hours. Remove cover and stir the meat and marinade occasionally. Replace cover and continue to refrigerate.

2. Place cubes of meat on wooden skewers. Each skewer should contain about eight pieces. The meat cubes should clearly be touching but not crowded. Do not add vegetables to the same skewer as the meat; traditionally souvlaki are only made from meat or chicken cubes.

3. Place the souvlaki on a hot barbecue grill. Cook over moderate to high heat, turning constantly to create even color. Do not overcook. While barbecuing, the souvlaki may be basted with a mixture of olive oil, fresh lemon juice, crushed garlic and salt and pepper. Do not use the remaining marinade to baste the meat while cooking.

4. These delicious souvlaki are traditionally served with tzatziki dip, Greek salad, feta cheese, calamata olives and fresh Greek bread. However, a number of other dishes go very well, such as stuffed vine leaves, stuffed phyllo, hummus dip, tarama (caviar) dip and roasted peppers. Just about any dish you can think of works well as an accompaniment to lamb, chicken, pork or beef souvlaki. Wow!

Note: Vegetables may be placed on separate skewers and served with the meat souvlaki. Vegetables to use when making up a vegetable skewer are red, green or yellow sweet bell peppers, onion pieces, mushrooms and unpeeled eggplant pieces.

GROUND SIRLOIN AND NUTTY WHITE RICE SERVED WITH PLAIN YOGHURT AND CUCUMBER SALAD

1 lb	extra lean ground sirloin or extra lean ground lamb	450 grams
1/4 cup	white onion, very finely chopped	180 mL
1/2 cup	toasted pine nuts, chopped	125 mL
2 cloves	crushed garlic	
2 tbsp	extra virgin olive oil	30 mL
1 tbsp	butter	15 mL
2 tsp	fresh ground cinnamon powder	10 mL
2 tsp	fresh ground allspice powder	10 mL
1 tsp	fresh ground black pepper	5 mL
1 tsp	salt (optional)	5 mL
3 cups	fully cooked, white rice	750 mL
2 1/2 cups	plain, unflavored yoghurt	625 mL
1 1/2 cups	fresh, semi-peeled cucumber, finely chopped or diced	375 mL
1/2 cup	chopped fresh parsley, chopped finely	125 mL

METHOD:

1. In a non-stick pan containing olive oil, sauté the ground meat and onion. Add 2 cloves of crushed garlic and toasted pine seeds. (Pan toast the pine seeds in 1 tbsp melted butter until a deep golden brown color). Add to the meat and onion mixture. Add spices and cooked rice. Carefully combine all of the ingredients together.

2. Combine plain yoghurt, 2 cloves of crushed garlic and chopped cucumber. Blend ingredients together. Refrigerate for about 1 hour before serving.

3. Serve rice and meat mixture as a main dish with yoghurt and cucumber salad. Sprinkle with chopped fresh parsley. This dish is ideally served with roast chicken or any meat. It also makes a great stuffing for chicken or turkey on its own, excluding the yoghurt of course.

ROAST YOUNG CHICKEN MARINATED IN FRESH ROSEMARY AND GARLIC

2 2 1/2 lb	fresh whole chickens	2 - 1 kg chickens
1/2 cup	extra virgin olive oil	125 mL
4 cloves	crushed garlic	
2 tsp	fresh ground black pepper	10 mL
2 tsp	Hungarian paprika	10 mL
2 tsp	salt (optional)	10 mL
1/2 cup	fresh rosemary (remove and discard stem)	125 mL

METHOD:

1. Thoroughly wash and dry the chickens. Remove the leaves from the stem of the rosemary plant. Discard the stem and place the leaves in a food processor and blend until they are very finely chopped.

2. Combine chopped rosemary, olive oil, crushed garlic and spices. Blend all ingredients together, making a paste. Coat the entire surface of both chickens with the marinade, using your hands. Use all of the marinade. Cover and place in the refrigerator for at least six hours.

3. Place the chickens on the rack of a roasting pan. Bake at 375° F or 190° C for approximately 2 - 2 1/2 hours or until the chickens are golden brown and tender. Baste regularly with a mixture of 1/2 cup or 125 mL chicken stock, 2 tbsp or 30 mL melted butter and 1/2 tsp or 3 mL of paprika.

4. When chickens are tender, remove from the oven and serve with vegetable rice pilaf, any potato dish, baked eggplant and feta cheese casserole, a favorite salad or roasted peppers and feta stuffed phyllo. Delicious!

SEASONED, (OVEN-BAKED) FRIED CHICKEN

12	chicken pieces, any favorite pieces may be used	
4 cups	dry bread crumbs	1 litre
2	whole eggs, well beaten	
1 cup	fresh milk	250 mL
3 tsp	garlic powder	15 mL
2 tsp	dry oregano flakes	10 mL
2 tsp	Hungarian paprika	10 mL
2 tsp	fresh ground black pepper	10 mL
1 tsp	salt (optional)	10 mL
4 tbsp	light olive oil or canola oil	60 mL

METHOD:

1. Wash and dry the chicken pieces. Skin may be removed. Combine milk and eggs and beat until foamy.

2. Combine bread crumbs with spices. Use the crumbs only as needed, do not use them all at once. Dip the chicken pieces into the milk and egg mixture and roll in seasoned bread crumbs. Ensure that the chicken is completely coated.

3. Place the chicken pieces in a greased baking pan. When all of the chicken pieces are in the pan, drizzle the tops with olive oil or canola oil. Bake at 450° F or 230° C for approximately 45 minutes or until the chicken is golden brown and crisp on all sides. Turn the chicken two or three times, using tongs, during baking to ensure even browning. Remove from the oven and serve hot or cold. Serve with potatoes or rice and a salad for a delicious meal. Great for picnics, snacks and lunches!

TRADITIONAL, SLOW ROASTED LEG OF LAMB WITH FRESH OREGANO

Marinade

1/2 cup	extra virgin olive oil	125 mL
1/4 cup	fresh squeezed lemon juice (not bottled)	60 mL
1/4 cup	fresh oregano leaves, finely chopped	
2 tsp	salt	10 mL
2 tsp	dry mint	10 mL
2 tsp	fresh ground black pepper	10 mL
2 cloves	crushed garlic	
1/4 cup	dry red wine (optional)	60 mL
1 - 5 lb	leg of local lamb (shoulder may be used)	approximately 2 kg
2 tsp	Hungarian paprika	10 mL
2 tsp	salt	10 mL
3 cups	cold water	
12	small, white potatoes	

All of the above are approximately measurements only. The combination of ingredients shoul remain the same, however the quantities may vary according to individual preferences.

METHOD:

1. Thoroughly wash the lamb with cold water. Remove any excess fat from the meat. Do not remove all of the fat, however, as a small amount is required to keep the meat moist while roasting. Using a sharp knife, scrape the surface of the roast on all sides to remove any impurities. Rewash the meat with cold water. This scraping will leave the surface of the meat slightly rough. The rough surface will enable the marinade to be more easily absorbed.

2. Combine all the ingredients of the marinade. Pour the marinade over the meat and turn the meat so that all sides are coated. Cover tightly and refrigerate for at least eight hours. Place the lamb in a large roasting pan. Pour the remaining marinade over the roast. Sprinkle the meat with an additional 2 tsp of salt, 2 tsp

paprika and 1 tsp fresh ground black pepper. Add about 3 cups of cold water to the bottom of the roasting pan. Cover tightly and roast in a 375 degree F or 190 degree C oven for approximately three hours. Baste the roast often with the juices from the roast that collect at the bottom of the pan. Remove from the oven and arrange the potatoes around the meat. Sprinkle the potatoes with paprika, dry oregano flakes and salt and pepper. Baste the meat and continue to bake, uncovered, for another hour or until the potatoes have browned and the meat is very soft and tender. If the meat is not soft enough, baste again and continue to bake for an additional $1/2$ hour. The meat should be golden brown on the surface and very tender and juicy on the inside. Cover the roast tightly for about 15 minutes before serving. Gravy may be made by combining 2 tbsp butter and 3 tbsp flour in a saucepan. Using a whisk and beating constantly add 2 cups of light beef or vegetable stock. Add all the drippings from the roast and whisk until gravy thickens. Slice the roast and place on a serving platter surrounded by the roast potatoes. Drizzle with the gravy. Serve with any of your favorite side dishes, but cold plain yoghurt is a must!

DESSERTS

About Dessert

The word "dessert," as we know it in North America, means something sweet that is served as the final course, completing a meal. It usually consists of some type of cake or pastry, pudding, ice cream or a combination thereof. Traditionally in Greece, as in many other parts of the world as well, "sweets" are not eaten in this fashion. In Greece, specifically, cakes and pastries are eaten only on special occasions, not at the end of a daily meal. The type of food most commonly eaten as their "dessert" is fresh fruit. Fresh fruit is traditionally served at the end of each large meal, such as lunch or dinner and is often eaten as the main course, especially for breakfast and lunch. They tend to eat whatever fruit is in season, ranging from watermelon and cantaloupe to pomegranates, black, red or green grapes, apples, pears, peaches, cherries, oranges, lemons, black and red plums and fresh figs.

Sweets, such as those recipes offered in this cookbook are recipes which are prepared for holidays and special occasions, such as Christmas, New Year, name sake days, and birthdays. They are prepared for weddings, engagements and the birth of a baby. Although the Greek pastries traditionally eaten, which recipes are offered herein, may, in some cases, seem very rich and sweet, keep in mind that they are prepared and eaten, only occasionally.

Baklava

2 packages	phyllo dough	
1 lb	unsalted butter	450 grams
3 cups	fresh shelled walnuts (not packaged)	750 mL
Syrup		
4 cups	cold water	1 litre
4 cups	granulated white sugar	1 litre
2 tbsp	fresh squeezed lemon juice (not bottled)	30 mL
1 tsp	fresh ground cinnamon powder	5 mL

METHOD:

1. Melt the butter slowly over low heat. Set aside to cool. In a large, rectangular baking pan approximately 12 in. or 30 cm. x 16 in. or 40 cm. x 2 in. or 4 cm., which has been buttered using 2 tbsp or 30 mL of the melted butter, place one package of phyllo dough. Do not separate the sheets, use the entire package as it comes. Trim the phyllo dough carefully to fit the pan.

2. Place shelled nuts in a food processor and using the "Pulse" button, chop the nuts until they are very fine and granular. If the pieces are not fine enough, it will be difficult to cut the baklava. Spread nuts over phyllo. Reserve 1/4 cup. Immediately, place the second package of phyllo over the nuts. Trim the dough once again to fit the pan. Phyllo must be room temperature when using. If cold, it will break and cannot be used. Keep it in the plastic packages and remove it only when you are ready to use it.

3. Using a very sharp knife, carefully cut 1 1/2 in. or 4 cm. strips in the baklava, from one end to the other. Hold the surrounding phyllo dough with one hand while cutting with the other and work as quickly as possible, before the dough dries and breaks. Immediately turn the pan and again cut strips in the opposite direction, creating either squares, or traditional diamond shapes. Diamond shapes can be achieved by cutting the second set of strips on a slight angle in the pan. This must be done very carefully. The baklava should be cut right through to the bottom of the pan, but does not have to be exact as it will be cut again before serving. The purpose of the cutting at this point is because the baklava is impossible to cut after baking, as it is crisp and dry at that point and would crumble. Using a small ladle, carefully drizzle all of the melted butter over the cut baklava. Try to target the lines where it has been cut as well as the edges first, but all of the baklava must be covered with the butter. Gently tip the pan from side to side until the butter has been absorbed. Bake at 300° F or 150° C for about 1 hour. Cheek after 45 minutes but try not to open the oven until then, as it affects the rising process. Baklava is ready when it has puffed up, pulled away from the sides of the pan and is light golden brown. Remove from oven and allow to cool at room temperature. When baklava is cool, drizzle with cooled syrup (recipe follows). Allow to sit in the pan for 12 hours before serving. The syrup will have saturated the baklava but it will still have a crisp texture. This traditional Greek pastry will delight you!

HOME-MADE SYRUP FOR BAKLAVA

4 cups	cold water	1 litre
4 cups	granulated, white sugar	1 litre
2 tbsp	fresh squeezed lemon juice (not bottled)	30 mL
1 tsp	fresh ground cinnamon powder	5 mL

METHOD:

1. Combine cold water, sugar and lemon juice in a large, deep saucepan. Add cinnamon powder and stir over high heat until the sugar and the cinnamon are completely dissolved. Remove any undissolved particles of cinnamon. Stir until the mixture reaches a brisk, rolling boil. At this point, do not stir or put any utensil into the syrup until ready to pour over the baklava. Stirring during the boiling process changes the temperature and prevents the syrup from thickening.

2. Boil rapidly, uncovered over high heat for exactly 38 minutes. Remove from heat and allow to cool in the pot for about 3 hours. The water and sugar mixture will have reduced to about half the amount during the boiling process. You should have about 2 cups or 500 mL of syrup. When the syrup has cooled, drizzle it carefully and evenly over the cooled baklava, using a small ladle. It will appear as though the syrup is sitting on top of the baklava and is not being absorbed. This is normal. Allow the baklava and syrup to sit at room temperature in the original baking pan for at least 12 hours. At that point the syrup will have been completely absorbed. The baklava will, however, still have a slightly crispy consistency. Very carefully, re-cut the pieces of baklava and remove gently. Serve with coffee or tea as a dessert. Your friends and family will be amazed!

Note: Although walnuts are traditionally used for baklava, my own personal variation seems to have won recognition and become a definite favorite of my own family and friends. Being a lover of pecans in almost any variation, I decided that substituting traditional walnuts for pecans would work well; and work well it did! The incredibly rich, praline flavor that is derived from the crushed pecans when combined with the buttery flavor of the baked phyllo, together with the rich caramel flavor of the cinnamon syrup, gives birth to a taste creation that in my opinion, truly rivals generations of tradition. If you enjoy the flavor of pecans, my Pecan Baklava will astound you!

APPLE, PECAN
AND RAISIN CINNAMON STRUDEL

8-10	large, tart apples, peeled, cored and cut into very thin wedges	
1/2 cup	fresh shelled pecans, chopped finely	125 mL
1/2 cup	raisins	125 mL
3 tsp	fresh ground cinnamon powder	25 mL
2 cups	firmly packed, light brown sugar	500 mL
1/4 cup	melted, unsalted butter	60 mL
2 tbsp	flour	30 mL
1 package	phyllo dough (room temperature)	

METHOD:

1. When making strudel, work on a clean, flat surface, covered with a large tea towel or tablecloth. Lightly flour the surface and place the phyllo sheets directly on the floured towel or tablecloth. Using this method makes the rolling process of the phyllo dough much easier and prevents breaking or tearing. Use 4 sheets of phyllo dough for each strudel. Take 2 sheets of phyllo and place them flat with the horizontal measurement being greater than the vertical. Brush the entire surface with melted butter and place two additional sheets on top of the first two.

2. Place the peeled, sliced apples in a large bowl. Add brown sugar, pecans, raisins and cinnamon. Blend the ingredients together. Sprinkle in the flour and blend thoroughly. Count the phyllo dough in groups of four and decide how many strudels you will be making. Divide the apple filling accordingly. Place the filling along the wide edge of the phyllo, closest to you. Spread the filling evenly, leaving about 1 in. or 2 1/2 cm. at each end of the dough. There should be a generous portion of filling for each strudel. Lift the bottom of the cloth closest to you and roll the phyllo, carefully, in a jelly roll fashion. Securely tuck the ends of the dough under and place the strudel on a buttered baking pan. Continue this with the remaining phyllo, in sheets of four, and the remaining filling. Brush the entire surface of each strudel, generously with the melted butter. Bake at 350° F or 175° C for approximately 35 minutes or until the strudel is golden brown. Remove from oven. When the strudel has cooled, slice it diagonally and sprinkle each portion with powdered sugar. Delicious with ice cream.

STRAWBERRY AND CHEESE STRUDEL

1 ¹/2 cups	pure strawberry jam (strawberry may be substituted with any other pure fruit jam)	325 mL
2 cups	ricotta cheese	500 mL
¹/2 cup	cream cheese	125 mL
2	whole eggs, well beaten	
¹/2 cup	granulated sugar	125 mL
¹/2 tsp	pure vanilla extract	3 mL
¹/4 cup	melted, unsalted butter	60 mL
1 package	phyllo dough (room temperature)	
powdered sugar mixed with unsweetened cocoa powder for decoration		

METHOD:

1. The method for preparing and rolling this strudel is the same as the method used for apple, pecan and raisin cinnamon strudel, previously shown. The difference is only in the preparation of the filling.

2. In a large bowl, combine ricotta cheese, cream cheese, sugar and vanilla. Beat with an electric beater until smooth and creamy. Add eggs and continue to beat until all ingredients are well blended, about 2 minutes. Beat with an electric beater until smooth and creamy. Using four sheets of phyllo per strudel with butter between the center layers, spread the cheese filling about 3/4 in. or 2 cm. thick, along the wide edge of the phyllo closest to you. Leave about 1 in. or 2 ¹/2 cm. at each end. Dab the jam, randomly over the cheese mixture. Lift the bottom of the cloth closest to you and roll the phyllo, carefully, in a jelly roll fashion. Carefully tuck the ends of the dough under and place the strudel on a buttered baking pan. Continue with remaining phyllo in groups of four sheets, and the remaining filling. Brush the entire surface of each strudel, generously with the melted butter. Bake at 350° F or 175° C for approximately 35 minutes or until the strudel is golden brown. Remove from the oven. When the strudel has cooled, slice, diagonally and sprinkle with powdered sugar mixed with unsweetened cocoa powder.

DELICATE PECAN ORANGE CAKE

1/3 cup	unsalted butter	60 mL
1 cup	granulated sugar	250 mL
3 tsp	baking powder	15 mL
2 cups	cake flour	500 mL
3	whole eggs, well beaten	
3/4 cup	milk	180 mL
	rind of one orange	
1/2 cup	fresh shelled pecans, finely chopped	125 mL

Topping

	fresh squeezed juice from 2 large oranges	
	the peel from one whole orange, grated	
	1 cup icing sugar	250 mL
1/2 tsp	orange blossom water	3 mL

METHOD:

1. Preheat oven to 350° F or 175° C.

2. In a large mixing bowl, cream the butter and add the sugar. Add eggs and beat until light and airy. Add dry ingredients to the butter and sugar mixture. Add milk Mix well. Add orange rind and pecan pieces. Pour into a well- buttered 9 in. or 3 litre bundt pan and bake 30 minutes or until cake springs back when pressed lightly. Cake will be light golden brown and fluffy. Insert a toothpick into the center of the cake; if it comes out dry, the cake is done. Remove from the oven and cool completely, before removing from the pan.

3. In a small bowl, squeeze the juice from two large oranges. Remove all seeds. Add the rind from one whole orange and icing sugar. Add orange blossom water. Mix thoroughly until the sugar is dissolved. Invert the cake on a decorative dish. Drizzle evenly with icing sugar and orange juice mixture. This cake may be refrigerated for about one hour before serving, if desired. A delightfully fresh and flavorful cake.

Succulent Banana Cake Muffins

1/4 cup	unsalted butter	180 mL
1 3/4 cups	granulated sugar, less sugar may be used	430 mL
2	whole eggs, slightly beaten	
2 cups	whole wheat cake flour	500 mL
3 tsp	baking powder	15 mL
2 tsp	pure vanilla extract	10 mL
1/4 cup	sour milk (milk with 1/2 tsp or 3 mL white vinegar added)	180 mL
1 1/4 cups	mashed, very ripe banana	310 mL

Method:

1. In a large bowl, beat butter until smooth, add sugar and eggs. Add mashed banana and vanilla extract. Combine dry ingredients in a separate bowl and gradually add to the butter mixture. Add the sour milk and mix with a wooden spoon or spatula, just until blended. Do not over mix. Spoon into buttered muffin tins. Fill tins 2/3 full.

2. Bake at 350° F or 175° C for about 12 - 15 minutes or until the muffins have risen and are golden brown. The tops of the muffins may split slightly when done. Do not open the oven during the baking process, as this inhibits the rising process.

3. Serve the muffins warm from the oven or cool. Delicious for breakfast, snacks and afternoon tea. Great for lunch boxes!

CREAMY RICE CUSTARD

2 cups	milk	500 mL
1 cup	cooked white rice	250 mL
2	egg yolks, beaten	
2	egg whites, beaten	
3/4 cup	sugar	180 mL
1 1/2 tsp	fresh ground cinnamon powder	8 mL
1/3 cup	raisins, light or dark may be used	160 mL
1 1/2 tsp	pure vanilla extract	8 mL
	fresh ground nutmeg for decoration	
	whipped cream for garnish (optional)	

METHOD:

1. Combine 2 cups of homogenized milk and 1 cup of cooked rice in the top of a double boiler and bring to a boil. In a separate bowl, combine egg yolks, cinnamon and sugar. Beat with a whisk until foamy. Add a small amount of rice and milk mixture to the beaten egg yolks. Mix well. Add the egg mixture back into the rest of the milk and rice. Simmer over low heat, stirring constantly until the mixture thickens. Remove from heat and cool to room temperature.

2. Beat egg whites with an electric beater until they peak. Add the vanilla and beat until blended. Fold the egg whites into the rice mixture, gradually. Scald raisins in 1 cup of boiling water. Drain and place on a paper towel to dry. Add the raisins and blend all ingredients together. Pour pudding into individual serving dishes. Place in refrigerator for at least 6 hours before serving or until cold. Garnish with whipped cream and a dash of fresh ground nutmeg.

Fluffy, Deep fried Fritters with Cinnamon Sugar

2 cups	all purpose white flour	500 mL
2	whole eggs, well beaten	
1 cup	warm water	250 mL
1/2 tsp	sugar	3 mL
1 tbsp	or 1 package, traditional dry yeast	15 mL
4 tbsp	granulated sugar	60 mL
1 1/2 cups	warm water or skim milk	375 mL
1 cup	granulated sugar	250 mL
2 tbsp	flesh ground cinnamon powder	30 mL
	canola oil for deep flying	

Method:

1. Add the yeast to one cup of warm water containing 1/2 tsp of sugar. Stir and set aside to rise for approximately 10 minutes. In a large bowl, combine the flour and 4 tbsp of granulated sugar. Add the risen yeast and the eggs. Add warm milk and stir well until all ingredients are blended. Your dough should have a slightly thick elastic consistency. This elasticity is because you are using all-purpose, or hard wheat flour. Cover the bowl containing the dough with a clean tea towel and allow to rise at room temperature for approximately a 1/2 hour. The dough will double in size. The dough should keep its shape when dropped from a spoon into hot oil.

2. Using a deep fryer or a deep stainless steel pot, heat canola oil. Drop a small amount of dough into the oil to test the temperature. Temperature of oil should be about 360° F or 175° C. The dough should immediately float to the surface of the hot oil and begin turning golden brown. Drop the dough from a small ladle into the hot oil. Four or five fritters may be deep fried at a time. Frying time for each fritter should be approximately 2 minutes, turning constantly. Browning too quickly is an indication that they are not cooking on the inside. The shapes will be irregular. Use the same amount of dough for each one, trying to keep them as uniform in shape, as possible. They will, however, all be slightly different. Remove fritters from hot oil and place on double paper towels to remove excess oil while cooling. Allow to cool for at least one hour. Place on a large platter and sprinkle generously with 1 cup of sugar mixed with 2 tbsp fresh ground cinnamon powder. These tasty treats are delicious with coffee or tea.

HOME-MADE APPLE SAUCE WITH CINNAMON AND RAISINS

6-8	large apples, any type of apples may be used	
1 cup	water	250 mL
1/2 cup	brown sugar	125 mL
1 tsp	fresh squeezed lemon juice	5 mL
1/4 cup	dark raisins	60 mL
1 1/2 tsp	fresh ground cinnamon powder	8 mL

METHOD:

1. Wash and core the apples. Apples may be peeled, or left unpeeled. Cut apples into chunks or wedges and place in a saucepan. Add about 1 cup of cold water, brown sugar, lemon juice, cinnamon and raisins.

2. Simmer over medium heat for about 20 minutes, stirring often, until the apples are very soft. Remove from heat and mash the apples down with a spoon. For a smoother applesauce, use a potato masher. Place in individual serving dishes and garnish with a sprinkle of fresh cinnamon powder. Refrigerate and serve cold as a delicious dessert. A great condiment when served with pork or chicken.

OLD-FASHIONED CINNAMON ROLLS

1 cup	warm milk	250 mL
2 tbsp	traditional dry yeast	30 mL
1/2 cup	granulated sugar	125 mL
1 tsp	salt	5 mL
1/4 cup	soft butter	60 mL
2	whole eggs, well beaten	
2 1/2 cups	all purpose flour	625 mL

Filling

3/4 cup	soft butter	180 mL
4 tbsp	fresh ground cinnamon powder	60 mL
1/4 cup	dark raisins (optional)	60 mL

METHOD:

1. Place warm milk and dry yeast in a large mixing bowl. Stir and allow to sit at room temperature for about five minutes until it has risen.

2. Add the sugar, salt, butter and eggs to the yeast, and beat with an electric mixer until creamy. Gradually add 1 1/2 cups of all purpose flour and continue beating until all ingredients are well blended. Cover the bowl with a clean tea towel and allow the dough to rise for about 45 minutes.

3. Add the remaining cup of flour and enough more flour to make the dough just barely firm enough to handle. Cover and chill about 35 minutes in the refrigerator. Remove the cold dough and roll out with a rolling pin, on a floured surface to 1/2 in. or 1 1/2 cm. thickness. Spread the surface of the rolled dough, evenly, with 3/4 cup of soft butter mixed with 4 tbsp of fresh ground cinnamon powder. Cover the entire surface of the dough. Sprinkle the raisins evenly over the dough. Rolling away from you, roll the dough in jolly roll fashion. You will end up with a long roll. Cut the dough in 1 1/2 in. or approximately 4 cm. slices, using a sharp knife. Place the unbaked rolls, pin wheel side up in a buttered baking pan. Be sure that the rolls are placed snugly in the pan and are touching. Cover with a tea towel and allow to proof at room temperature for about 1 hour.

Bake at 350° F or 175° C for approximately 20 minutes or until the rolls have risen and are golden brown. Remove from the oven and cool at room temperature for about a $1/2$ hour. Mix $1/4$ cup boiling water with confectioner's sugar. Add enough sugar to achieve the correct consistency to spread over the rolls. Add $1/2$ tsp or 3 mL of pure vanilla extract and blend thoroughly.

4. Using a wide knife or spatula, spread the frosting generously over each roll. Serve warm or cold. Great for breakfast, delicious any time!

FLUFFY, GOLDEN CORN MUFFINS

1 cup	cornmeal	250 mL
$3/4$ cup	cake flour	180 mL
$1/2$ cup	granulated sugar	125 mL
4 tsp	baking powder	20 mL
$1/2$ tsp	salt	3 mL
1 cup	milk	250 mL
2	whole eggs, beaten	
$1/4$ cup	butter, melted	60 mL

METHOD:

1. In a large bowl, combine the cornmeal, flour, baking powder, sugar and salt. Mix in the eggs, milk and melted butter. Mix just until blended. Do not over mix.

2. Fill buttered muffin pans $2/3$ full of the batter. Bake at 350° F or approximately 15 - 18 minutes or until the muffins are fluffy and golden brown.

3. Remove from the oven and serve warm or cool, with jam or jelly, or on their own. A delicious snack with coffee, tea, milk or juice.

SWEET CHEESE PIE MADE WITH SHREDDED PHYLLO PASTRY

1	package shredded phyllo pastry	
2 1/4 cup	ricotta cheese	560 mL
1	whole egg, well beaten	
3/4 cup	finely shredded mozzarella cheese	80 mL
1 lb	unsalted butter, melted	450 grams

toasted sliced almonds for garnish (pan toast over low heat until golden brown)

Syrup

2 cups	cold water	500 mL
2 cups	granulated sugar	500 mL
2 tsp	fresh squeezed lemon juice	10 mL
2 tbsp	rose water (available at most Mediterranean grocery stores)	30 mL

METHOD:

1. Combine sugar and cold water in a saucepan, and add the fresh lemon juice. Stir over high heat until the mixture comes to a boil and the sugar is completely dissolved. Add the rose water and stir. Once the sugar and water begins to boil, do not stir again. Any contact with the boiling liquid will lower the temperature and will prevent the syrup from thickening. Boil rapidly for 15 minutes. Remove from heat and cool to room temperature.

2. Coat the shredded pastry with melted, slightly cooled butter. Place half of the coated pastry, evenly over the bottom of a baking pan 12 in. or 30 cm. x 10 in. or 25 cm. by 1 in. or 2 1/2 cm. Combine ricotta cheese and shredded mozzarella cheese in a food processor and add the egg. Beat until the ingredients are well blended and have a smooth texture. Spread the cheese evenly over the bottom layer of pastry. Cover the cheese, evenly, with the remaining coated phyllo dough. Bake in a preheated 350° F oven for about 30 - 35 minutes or until the pastry becomes golden brown. Remove from oven and cool at room temperature.

3. Drizzle the cheese pie with 1 cup of cooled syrup. Refrigerate before serving. Cut into individual serving portions and drizzle with additional syrup. Sprinkle with toasted sliced almonds.

DATE FILLED ORANGE COOKIES

1/4 lb	unsalted butter, melted	225 grams
1/4 cup	granulated sugar	60 mL
1/4 cup	fresh squeezed orange juice (not frozen)	60 mL
1 tsp	baking powder	5 mL
1/4 tsp	fresh ground cinnamon powder	2 mL
2 cups	cake flour	500 mL

Date Filling

3/4 cup	cooked, mashed dates	180 mL
3/4 cup	cold water	180 mL
1/4 cup	dark brown sugar	60 mL
2 tsp	pure vanilla extract	10 mL
	confectioner's sugar for dusting	

METHOD:

1. Place pitted dates in a saucepan and add cold water, brown sugar and vanilla. Simmer over medium heat until all ingredients begin to blend together and mixture begins to boil. Reduce heat and continue to simmer until the water has been absorbed and the dates are soft and thick. Remove from heat and mash, using a potato masher until the dates are smooth. Allow to cool. Date mixture will thicken as it cools.

2. In a large bowl, combine melted butter, granulated sugar and cinnamon. Add the baking powder to the orange juice and stir into the butter and sugar mixture. Gradually add the flour. The dough should be firm enough to shape. Place a small amount, approximately 3 tbsp or 45 mL of dough in the palm of one hand. Flatten the dough into a circle, using the thumb of the other hand. Place about 1 tsp or 5 mL of the cooled date filling in the center of the dough. Carefully, bring the edges of the circle together, enclosing the date mixture in the center of the cookie. Shape into a finger or crescent shape. Bake at 350° F or 175° F for about 18 to 20 minutes, or until the cookie is golden brown. Remove from the oven and cool. Place the cookies on a decorative serving plate and dust with confectioner's sugar. Delicious with coffee, tea, milk or juice.

GOLDEN BISCUITS WITH FRESH CITRUS

3/4 lb	unsalted butter	180 mL
1 2/3 cups	granulated sugar	410 mL
4	whole eggs, beaten	
2 tsp	pure vanilla extract	10 mL
2 tbsp	whiskey (optional)	10 mL
1/2 tsp	baking soda	3 mL
2 1/2 tsp	baking powder	13 mL
2 tbsp	fresh lemon rind, finely grated	30 mL
4 1/2 cups	all purpose flour	just over 1 litre
3	egg yolks, well beaten,	
	sesame seeds (optional)	

METHOD:

1. Preheat oven to 350° F or 175° C Have all ingredients at room temperature.

2. Place butter in a large mixing bowl. Add sugar and eggs and beat until fluffy. Add vanilla, whiskey, and orange juice. Add baking soda, baking powder and lemon rind. Beat for approximately five minutes, using an electric beater. Stir in the flour, gradually, using a wooden spoon. Dough should be soft, yet firm enough to shape. Divide the dough and roll fingers about 4 in. or 10 cm. in length and about 1/2 in. or 1 1/4 cm. in width. Place three fingers parallel to each other on a flat surface. Pinch at one end, joining all three fingers together. Gently braid the dough, not too tightly and pinch again at the opposite end. Continue making these braid-shaped biscuits until all of the dough is used. Place biscuits on a greased cookie sheet and brush with beaten egg yolks. Sprinkle with sesame seeds and bake for approximately 20 minutes or until golden brown. Check the bottoms of the cookies to ensure they do not overcook. Remove from oven and cool at room temperature. Pretty to serve and delicious to eat.

BUTTER PECAN POUND CAKE

1 1/4 cups	unsalted butter	300 mL
4 tsp	baking powder	20 mL
2 1/4 cups	cake and pastry flour	550 mL
1 1/4 cups	granulated sugar	300 mL
3	egg yolks, well beaten	
1/2 cup	milk	125 mL
1/2 cup	evaporated milk	125 mL
1/4 cup	fresh, shelled pecans, chopped	60 mL
3	egg whites, beaten	
	confectioner's sugar for dusting	

METHOD:

1. Preheat oven to 375° F or 190° C. Cream butter and add the sugar. Blend together until light and fluffy. Add the dry ingredients, gradually into the butter and sugar mixture. Combine well. Add egg yolks and milk. Add the chopped pecans. Beat by hand with a wooden spoon until blended, about 2 minutes.

2. Beat egg whites with an electric beater until thick. Gently fold beaten egg whites into the batter. Pour into a 9 in. or 3 litres bundt pan. Bake for about 40 minutes or until cake is golden brown and pulls away from the sides of the pan. Remove from the oven and cool in the pan. When cake is cooled, remove from the pan and dust with confectioner's sugar.

BAKED APPLES WITH BROWN SUGAR, RAISINS AND CRUSHED WALNUTS

6	large, slightly tart apples	
1 cup	brown sugar, light or dark, firmly packed	250 mL
1/2 cup	pure, liquid honey	125 mL
1/4 cup	raisins, dark or light	60 mL
1/4 cup	chopped walnuts	60 mL
1 1/2 tsp	fresh ground cinnamon powder	8 mL
1/2 cup	cold water	125 mL

METHOD:

1. Wash and core the apples. Do not peel. Place the apples in a shallow baking pan. Pour the cold water around the apples. Combine brown sugar, honey, raisins and chopped nuts. Mixture will be runny. Spoon equal amount of the sugar and honey mixture into the center of the apples. Bake the apples at 375° F or 190° C for about 45 minutes or until they are are soft and the topping is golden and bubbly. Pears may be used in place of apples.

2. Remove from the oven. May be served warm, or placed in the refrigerator until cold. Serve plain or with vanilla ice cream.

WALNUT COOKIES WITH HONEY SYRUP GLAZE

1 lb	unsalted butter, melted and cooled	450 grams
1/2 cup	granulated sugar	125 mL
4 cups	pastry flour	1 litre
2/3 cup	fresh squeezed orange juice (not bottled)	180 mL
3 tsp	baking powder	15 mL
1/2 tsp	fresh ground cinnamon powder	5 mL
1/4 tsp	ground nutmeg	3 mL
1 1/2 cups	shelled walnuts, chopped	625 mL

Syrup

3 cups	cold water	750 mL
3 cups	granulated sugar	750 mL
1 cup	pure, liquid honey	250 mL

METHOD:

1. Preheat oven to 350° F or 175° C. Combine melted butter, sugar, cinnamon and nutmeg. Stir well. Add baking powder to orange juice and stir into the butter mixture. Dough should be firm enough to shape. Add additional flour if necessary. Take a small amount of dough in the palm of one hand, about 2 tbsp or 30 mL Flatten the dough in a circle shape, using the thumb of the opposite hand. Place a few nut pieces in the center of the dough and bring the edges of the circle together to enclose the walnuts. Roll to form a finger or crescent shape. Place on an ungreased cookie sheet. Bake for about 15 minutes or until golden brown. Remove from oven and cool.

2. Combine 3 cups of sugar, 3 cups of water and 1 cup of honey in a saucepan. Simmer over high heat until mixture comes to a boil. Continue to simmer over high heat for 20 minutes. Do not stir during the boiling process. Remove from heat and allow to cool. When the syrup is cooled, dip the baked, cooled cookies, one at a time into the syrup. Remove and sprinkle with finely crushed walnuts (The walnuts in this recipe may be substituted for pecans).

3. Cookies may be stored in a tightly covered, plastic container in refrigerator.

Almond Flavored Syrup Sponge Cake

9	eggs, separated	
1 cup	farina	250 mL
1/2 cup	ground almonds	125 mL
2 tsp	pure almond extract	10 mL

Syrup

4 cups	cold water	1 litre
4 cups	granulated sugar	1 litre
2 tbsp	fresh lemon juice	30 mL
1 tbsp	lemon rind, finely grated	15 mL

Method:

1. Heat oven to 375 degree F or 190° C. Beat egg whites until stiff. Fold in farina and ground almonds. Beat egg yolks until light. Fold beaten egg yolks into the egg white mixture, gently and pour into a 12 in. x 14 in. or 30 cm. x 36 cm. buttered pan. Bake for about 25 minutes or until light golden brown. Cake should spring back when lightly pressed in the center. Do not open the oven door while the cake is baking. Remove the cake from the oven and cool slightly. Cut the cake into 2 1/2 in. or 6 cm. squares and do not remove from the pan.

2. Combine cold water, fresh lemon juice and lemon rind in a saucepan. Stir until the sugar is dissolved. Bring to a boil over high heat and simmer for 30 minutes. Remove from the heat and cool. Drizzle the cool syrup over the cool cake in the pan. Allow to sit in the pan at room temperature until all the syrup has been absorbed. Refrigerate for at least 4 hours before serving. Serve cold. Sprinkle individual servings with icing sugar. This is a sweet and delicate cake with a distinct almond flavor. Delicious with coffee or tea.

REFRESHING LEMON SPONGE CAKE PUDDING

5	whole eggs	
1 1/2 cups	granulated sugar	325 mL
1 tsp	vanilla extract	5 mL
1 cup	cake flour	250 mL
2 1/2 tsp	baking powder	13 mL

Lemon Sauce

2 cups	granulated sugar	500 mL
3	egg yolks, well beaten	
1/3 cup	fresh squeezed lemon juice	160 mL
1 cup	cold water	150 mL
2 cups	boiling water	500 mL
4 tbsp	corn starch	60 mL

METHOD:

1. Preheat oven to 350° F or 175° C In a large bowl, beat 5 eggs with an electric beater until light and fluffy. Slowly add 1 1/2 cups of sugar and vanilla. Continue to beat for about 3 minutes. Sift the flour and baking powder together and fold into the egg mixture with a rubber spatula. Pour into a greased 9 in. x 13 in. or 23 cm. x 33 cm., well buttered pan. Bake for approximately 35 minutes until the cake is light golden brown and springs back when gently pressed down. Remove from the oven and cool.

2. Beat the egg yolks until light and fluffy. Place in the top of a double boiler and add lemon juice and 2 cups of sugar. Blend ingredients together. In a small bowl combine cold water and corn starch and mix thoroughly. Using a wire whisk, stir the egg and lemon juice mixture and add the corn starch and water. Continue to stir with the whisk and slowly add the boiling water. Cook over medium heat, stirring constantly until the lemon mixture thickens. When mixture reaches a full boil, remove from heat and cool slightly. Serve warm lemon sauce over the cooled sponge cake. This tasty dessert has a refreshing, tangy flavor.

INDEX

BREADS AND DOUGHS

Basic Pita Dough / 72

Home-made Crusty Greek Bread Traditional Method / 75

Traditional Easter Bread (Sweet Egg Loaf) / 77

DAIRY PRODUCTS AND MAYONNAISE

About feta cheese / 80

Creamy Home-Made Mayonnaise / 83

Dill Flavored Mayonnaise / 83

Home-made Plain Yoghurt (Traditional Greek Method) / 82

Home-made Tzatziki / 83

Home-made, Unripened Mild Cheese / 80

Roasted Garlic Flavored Mayonnaise / 84

Roasted Sweet Red Pepper Mayonnaise / 84

Smoked Salmon Flavored Mayonnaise / 84

VEGETARIAN DISHES

Lemony - Traditional Stewed Greek Potatoes / 86

Vegetarian Moussaka with Potatoes, Eggplant and Zucchini / 87

Béchamel Sauce / 88

Baked Vegetable Casserole with Pine Nutty Rice / 89

Fluffy Mashed Potatoes with Caramelized Leeks / 90

Sautéed Fresh Green Beans with Caramelized Onions / 91

Delicious Leek and Potato Pancakes / 92

Lentils with Caramelized Onions and White Rice / 93

Baked Eggplant and Feta Cheese Casserole / 94

Baked Red Kidney Bean Casserole with Nutty Rice / 93

Barbecued Fresh Sardines Wrapped in Grape Vine Leaves with Olive Oil and Fresh Lemon / 96

Savory Greek Pizza with Browned Eggplant, Red and Yellow Peppers and Black Olives / 97

Fried Eggplant with Garlic and Lemon / 98

Spinach and Ricotta Cheese Lasagne / 99

Mouth-watering Falafel on Pita Bread with Fresh Veggies and Tahini Sauce / 100

Crunchy, Fresh Vegetable and Tahini Sauce for Falafel / 101

MAIN COURSES

Baked Chicken Breasts with Crushed Walnuts and Red Wine / 134

Baked Lamb and Fresh Okra Stew / 139

Baked Lamb and Summer Vegetable Medley / 112

Baked Lamb Stew with Orzo and Sweet Red and Yellow Peppers / 129

Baked Sole Fillets with Vegetable Medley Sauce / 145

Basic Greek Marinade / 105

Béchamel Sauce for Moussaka / 128

Broiled Cod Fillets with Garlic Butter and Fresh Parsley Fresh, Boneless Cod Fillets / 110

Broiled Fillet of Sole with Savoury Salmon Stuffing / 107

Cabbage Rolls with Lean Ground Meat and White Rice in Savory Tomato Sauce / 140

Chicken and Eggplant Ptarmigan with Portobello Mushrooms / 131

Chicken Breasts with Spicy Red Onion Sauce / 133

Colorful Chicken and Rice Pilaf / 138

Easy and Delicious Meatball and Potato Casserole / 136

Greek Meat Balls in Tomato Sauce / 148

Greek Style Chile / 120

Ground Lamb Meat Loaf with Sautéed Pepper, Tomato and Garlic Sauce / 121

Ground Sirloin and Nutty White Rice Served with Plain Yoghurt and Cucumber Salad / 150

Marinated Baby Lamb Chops / 126

Marinated Salmon Fillets with Garlic and Fresh Dill / 108

Moussaka with Ground Beef, Sliced Potatoes and Eggplant / 127

Pot Roast of Beef / 144

Red Chicken Rice Pilaf / 118

Rice Pilaf / 117

Roast Young Chicken Marinated in Fresh Rosemary and Garlic / 151

Salted Cod Fish with Spicy Red Rice Pilaf Casserole / 135

Savory Tomato Sauce / 142

Seafood Croquettes with Spicy Hot Banana Pepper Sauce / 110

Seasoned (Oven-Baked) Fried Chicken / 152

Souvlaki! Souvlaki! Souvlaki! / 149

Stuffed Baby Eggplants with Ground Lamb, White Rice and Pine Nuts / 111

Stuffed Bell Peppers with Ground Beef, Nutty Rice / 125

Succulent Roasted Pork Tenderloin with Fresh Leeks and Prunes / 1462

Tangy Stuffed Grape Leaves with Fresh Ground Lamb and White Rice / 114

Tender Beef and Caramelized Onion Casserole / 106

Tender Pork Spare Ribs and Kidney Bean Stew / 137

Traditional Baked Lamb with Fresh Spinach Casserole / 116

Traditional Baked Macaroni and Ground Beef Casserole / 123

Traditional Short Ribs of Beef with Vegetables / 140

Traditional, Slow Roasted Leg of Lamb with Fresh Oregano / 153

Vegetable Red Rice Pilaf / 119

Vegetable White Rice Pilaf / 118

DESSERTS

Almond Flavored Syrup Sponge Cake / 174

Apple, Pecan and Raisin Cinnamon Strudel / 159

Baked Apples with Brown Sugar, Raisins and Crushed Walnuts / 172

Baklava / 156

Butter Pecan Pound Cake / 171

Creamy Rice Custard / 163

Date Filled Orange Cookies / 169

Delicate Pecan Orange Cake / 161

Fluffy, Deep Fried Fritters with Cinnamon Sugar / 164

Fluffy, Golden Corn Muffins / 167

Golden Biscuits with Fresh Citrus / 170

Home-made Apple sauce with Cinnamon and Raisins / 165

Home-made Syrup for Baklava / 158

Old-Fashioned Cinnamon Rolls / 166

Refreshing Lemon Sponge Cake Pudding / 175

Strawberry and Cheese Strudel / 160

Succulent Banana Cake Muffins / 162

Sweet Cheese Pie Made with Shredded Phyllo Pastry / 168

Walnut Cookies with Honey Syrup Glaze / 173

A NOTE FROM THE AUTHOR

I feel privileged to be in a position to help. Through my work over the past four years, it has been my pleasure to support breast cancer research, both in Canada, by donating to the *National Breast Cancer Fund*, and in the United States, by donating to *The Breast Cancer Fund*. Breast cancer is every woman's issue, not only women who have tragically been stricken by this terrible disease, but every woman. I believe it is our duty to take breast cancer personally. I am a woman, I have three daughters, I take breast cancer personally. For this reason, I have chosen to do what I can to contribute to research being done both in Canada and in the United States, in the search for a cure for breast cancer. A portion of the proceeds from each and every sale of *Here's To Life* will be donated to The Breast Cancer Fund in the United States, or to the *National Breast Cancer Fund* in Canada.